✠

COPTIC ORTHODOX PATRIARCHATE

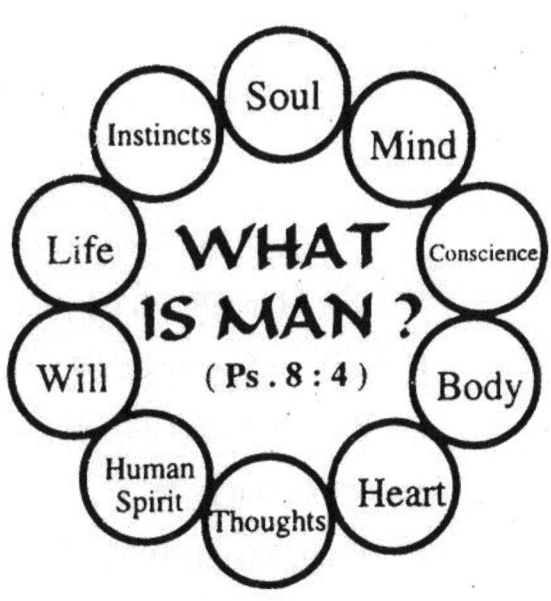

By
H. H. Pope Shenouda III

Title	: What is Man (Ps . 8 : 4) .
Author	: H. H. Pope Shenouda III .
Translated By	: Dr. Wedad Abbas .
Illustrated By	: Sister Sawsan .
Edition	: 1st Print, March 1997.
Typesetting	: Y. M . Ekladious .
Press	: Dar El Tebaa El-Kawmia .
Legal Deposit No.	: 8593/1996 .

H.H. Pope Shenouda III
117th Pope and Patriarch of Alexandria and the See of St Mark

INTRODUCTION

What is man?

This question was asked by David the Prophet in Psalm (8), where he said to the Lord, *"What is man that You are mindful of him"*, who, *"You have made him to have dominion over the works of Your hands; You have put all things under his feet"* (Ps. 8: 4, 6). David the Prophet spoke also about the end of man on the earth; he said in another psalm, *"Certainly every man at his best state is but vapor. Surely every man walks about like a shadow"* (Ps. 39: 5, 6).

St. James the apostle answered the question, *"What is your life?"*, *"It is even a vapor that appears for a little time and then vanishes away"* (Jas. 4: 14).

What is man, then?

Man is body, soul, and spirit (1 Thess. 5: 23).

Man is a soul having desires, and a spirit in touch with God: prays, contemplates, worships, and *"lusts against the flesh; and these are contrary to one another"* (Gal. 5: 17).

Man is a combination of instincts and capabilities, which he sometimes rules over and direct, and in other times his instincts prevail over him and lead his capabilities.

Man is a conscience giving rules, watching, judging and condemning.

Man is that giant intellect that made the spaceships that flew to the moon and still fly around the earth, observing and photographing.

Man is a heart throbbing with sentiments and emotions; sometimes they make him cry, and in other times they are harsh and turn him into a predatory animal.

Man is unceasing mind, with varied thoughts of different levels which might go high even unto heaven and unto God, or go very low as to be confined only to the flesh and material. Sometimes man's thoughts become entangled when they search matters above their level.

Man is all this together.

However, not all these matters are equal in man; for often one or more constituent prevails and becomes the distinctive characteristic for him. These constituents may also conflict, and the conflict continue or calm down. In this one differs from the other.

As some people said, man is "Micro Kosmos" i.e. a small world.

In this world, there are the high mountains, the deep sea, the mud and the swamps.
There are the gold and the jewels, the sand and the pebbles.
There are the shining light, and the mist that obscures light.

There are various things that are sometimes in harmony and other times contradicting.

Many sermons on man and his constituents were delivered by us in the Great Cathedral in Cairo.

Besides, twenty articles were published on the same subject in Watani Newspaper.

All this is then collected to form this book for you, dear reader, in an attempt to give an answer to the question: What is man?

There will be another book I hope to publish - God willing - on "Spirits".

Pope Shenouda III

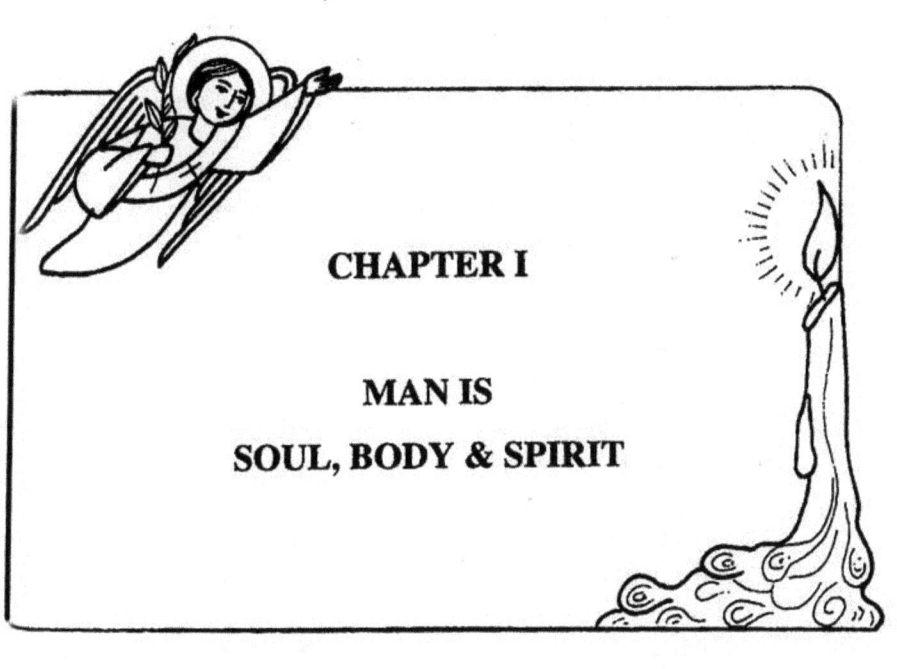

CHAPTER I

MAN IS SOUL, BODY & SPIRIT

WHAT IS MAN?

Body, Spirit & Soul:

Man is body, spirit and soul as we know from the Holy Bible and the church prayers.

1. St. Paul the Apostle says, *"May your whole spirit, soul, and body be preserved blameless at the coming of our Lord Jesus Christ..."* (1 Thess. 5: 23). Here, St. Paul mentioned the body, the spirit and the soul. The body need no explanation but,

2. **To distinguish between the soul and the spirit we bring the following evidences:**

    * St. Jude in his epistle says about the wicked, *"These are sensual persons... not having the Spirit"* (Jude 19).

    They behave according to the soul and senses not according to the spirit.

    * St. Paul the Apostle distinguished also between the soul and the spirit, saying, *"For the word of God is living and powerful, and sharper than any two-edged sword, piercing even to the division of soul and spirit"* (Heb. 4:12)

3. In the Holy Mass, we pray, saying, [Sanctify our souls, bodies and spirits.]

We say also about partaking of the Holy Sacraments that they are [A sanctification of our souls, bodies and spirits.]

4. **The spiritual fathers in their asceticism make the same distinction.**

They distinguish between living at the fleshly level and at the level of the soul or the spirit (refer to our book "Life of Virtue and Righteousness")

5. **Here we mention also, in the context of distinguishing between soul and spirit, that:**

Ancient Egyptians believed in "Ka" & "Ba". "Ka" means spirit (the plural "Kaw" means spirits.) So, the name of the King who built the third pyramid was "Man 'Kaw' Raa" which means the immortal spirits of Raa.

The word "Ba" equals "soul" in our language. God first created man from the dust of the ground. The dust became body, and God breathed into his nostrils the breath of life. This breath is the human spirit not the Holy Spirit as some wrongly think because if God had united in hypostasis with the body of man, man would have never sinned.

Let's now speak about the components of man: the soul, the spirit and the body:

The Soul:

There is a difference between the soul and the spirit.

The soul gives life to the body, but the spirit gives the person life with God. Therefore, animals have souls not spirits like humans. Our spirits are immortal, whereas animals have no immortal spirits.

And because the soul gives life to the body, the Book of Leviticus says, *"For the life of the flesh is in the blood"* (Lev. 17: 11, 14).

That is why God prohibited eating the blood, He said, *"You shall not eat the blood of any flesh, for the life of all flesh is its blood. Whoever eats it shall be cut off"* (Lev. 17: 14), and, *"No one among you shall eat blood, nor shall any stranger who sojourns among you eat blood"* (Lev. 17: 12).

This prohibition from eating blood started since the days of our father Noah.

When God permitted humans to eat flesh, he prohibited them from eating blood. He said, *"Every moving thing that lives shall be food for you. I have given you all things, even as the green herbs. But you shall not eat flesh with its life, that is, its blood"* (Gen. 9: 3,4)

This prohibition continued in the New Testament. When the father apostles decided to accept the Gentiles into faith, they sent them a letter, saying, *"... you abstain from things offered to idols, from blood, from things strangled, and from sexual immorality"* (Acts 15: 29)

Man's life is in the blood; if his blood is shed his life ends, his soul ends.

Someone may say that the death of a person means the death of the brain; that the brain with all its components stop to work, and this is followed by the death of the heart which means that the pulse of the heart stops.

In fact, this does not contradict with what we said. For when someone's blood is shed, the blood does not reach the brain, so it dies. Likewise, the heart cannot find blood to pump, so the pulse stops. Then the lungs stop respiration and man's last breath comes out.

As man's life is in the blood, blood was used to atone for sins; that is, a life taken instead of another.

Hence, the Lord God says, *"For the life of the flesh is in the blood, and I have given it to you upon the altar to make atonement for your souls; for it is the blood that makes atonement for the soul"* (Lev. 17: 11). That is why the blood was to be sprinkled all around the altar, on the horns of the altar or at the side or the base of the altar. (Lev. 1: 5, 11, 15); (Lev. 3: 2, 8); (Lev. 4: 29, 30, 34). The people never ate from it.

The three significances of the soul:

1. The first significance of the soul is its being the source of life to man, and that man's life is in his blood; if his blood is shed he dies.

2. The soul means the whole man:

* When God created man, He *"breathed into his nostrils the breath of life; and man became a living being"* (Gen. 2: 7)

* Speaking about those who were saved from the flood by the Ark, St. Peter the apostle said, *"... in which a few, that is, eight souls, were saved through water"* (1 Pet. 3: 20). By eight souls, St. Peter meant eight persons.

* About the children of Jacob who came to Egypt, the Book of Genesis says they were sixty six souls, i.e., persons (the two words are used alternatively in the various translations.)

* And King of Sodom, after the victory in the war with Chedorlaomer and the kings who were with him, said to our father Abraham *"Give me the souls* (in some translations: the persons), *and take the goods for yourself"* (Gen. 14: 21).

* The same was meant by the Lord when He said, *"learn from Me, for I am gentle and lowly in heart, and you will find rest for your souls"* (Mt. 11: 29); that is, to find rest for yourselves.

* The same goes with the words of St. James in his epistle. *"he who turns a sinner from the error of his way will save a soul from death and cover a multitude of sins"* (Jas. 5: 19), that is, will save the sinner himself.

* Concerning the punishment of those who ate leavened bread, the soul (or the person) who ate it was to be cut off from the congregation (Ex. 12: 19).

* And about the blood ordered to be given on the altar, God said *"it is the blood that makes atonement for the soul"*; that is, for the person.

* In the Book of Ezekiel, the Lord God said, *"The soul who sins shall die"* (Ezek. 18: 20). It means that the person who sins shall die.

3. By "the soul" is sometimes meant "the spirit".

* In the Parable of the Rich Fool who said, *"I will pull down my barns and build greater, and there I will store all my crops and my goods. And I will say to my soul, 'Soul, you have many goods laid up for many years...',"* God said to him, *"You fool! This night your soul will be required of you; then whose will those things be which you have provided?"* God meant that the spirit of that rich man would be taken from him and he would die. For it is the spirit that goes out and the person dies as the Lord Christ said on the Cross, *"Father, into Your hands I commend My spirit"* (Lk. 23: 46), and as St. Stephen said while being stoned, "Lord Jesus, receive my spirit" (Acts 7: 59).

* The word "soul" is used also by the Lord to mean "spirit" when He said, *"And do not fear those who will kill the body but cannot kill the soul. But rather fear Him who is able to destroy both soul and body in hell"* i.e. spirit and body.

The Body:
A note worth mentioning is that the body is not itself evil.

1. Had the body been evil, God would not have created it because God does not create evil things. When God created man as a body He saw that it was very good (Gen. 1: 26-31).

2. Had the body been an evil thing, the Lord God would not have taken body and become incarnate (Jn. 1: 14). It is impossible to say that the body of the Lord Christ was an evil thing!! The angel who announced to the Virgin the birth of the Lord Christ said to her, *"that Holy One who is to be born will be called the Son of God"* (Lk. 1: 35).

3. Had the body been an evil thing, God would not have aroused it from death. He would let it be eaten by worms, turn into dust and come to an end!

4. Had the body been and evil thing, no miracles would have occurred through bodies such as the dead person who arose when he touched the bones of Elisha the prophet (2 Kgs. 13: 21). Another example is the handkerchiefs and aprons brought from the body of St. Paul the apostle and put on the sick and the diseases left them and the evil spirit wen out of them (Acts 19: 12).

* The body is not evil in itself, otherwise we would not venerate the bodies and relics of saints and seek their blessing.
* The body is not evil in itself, because it participates with the spirit in worship. The spirit feels awe and the body bows and prostrates with it; the spirit addresses God in prayer and the body lifts the hands and eyes upwards and says with David the Prophet, *"The lifting up of my hands as the evening sacrifice"* (Ps. 141: 2); and *"I will lift up my hands in Your*

name. *My soul shall be satisfied as with marrow and fatness"* (Ps. 63: 4,5).

* Had the body been evil, the apostle would not have said, "... *glorify God in your body and in your spirit, which are God's"* (1 Cor. 6: 20).

* Had the body been evil, it would not have been a temple of the Holy Spirit as the apostle told us, *"Or do you not know that your body is the temple of the Holy Spirit who is in you"* (1 Cor. 6:19); *"Do you not know that you are the temple of God and that the Spirit of God dwells in you?"* (1 Cor. 3:16).

* Had the body been evil, the person who gives food to someone hungry would not have been considered to have given food to the Lord Christ Himself as He said: *"I was hungry and you gave Me food"* (Mt. 25:35).

* Had the body been evil, the Lord Christ would not have healed the sick nor praised the Good Samaritan who took care of the wounded man (Lk. 10: 33, 34) nor said, *"Those who are well do not need a physician, but those who are sick"* (Mt. 9:12, Lk. 5:31).

Thus, the body is of evil in itself but only if it clings to the material and to the lusts of this world, resists the spirit and walks against it.

In this case, the fault is not with the body but with its deviation towards sins like adultery, greed, drunkness, narcotics and addiction; which sins are called in the Holy Bible, *"the lust of the flesh, the lust of the eyes, and the pride of life"* (1 Jn. 2:

16). The other senses also may deviate as the Wise Solomon said, *"The eye is not satisfied with seeing, not the ear filled with hearing"* (Eccl. 1: 8).

So, the defect is not in the body, but in the bad use of the body, as the apostle says, **"For the flesh lusts against the Spirit, and the Spirit against the flesh; and these are contrary to one another"** (Gal. 5:17).

So, the apostle says, *"Walk in the Spirit, and you shall not fulfill the lust of the flesh"* (Gal. 5:16). But not every body lusts against the Spirit; for there are some bodies that rise to the spiritual level and the body becomes spiritual in its desires and conduct.

In the general Resurrection we shall rise in spiritual bodies. (1 Cor. 15: 44)

It is the same body but in a kind of transfiguration. That is why it is called a glorified body as St. Paul the Apostle says about the Lord Christ in His Second Coming *"who will transform our lowly body that it may be conformed to His glorious body"* (Phil. 3: 21).

The spirit and the possibility of its falling:

The spirit is the origin of one's attachment to God. It is the source of man's love to God, longing to Him and attachment to Him. Spiritual prayers and contemplations come out of the spirit, and it is the spirit that leads the mind and the body also to God. It controls all the heart feelings in a spiritual way, so a person may walk in the spirit, in communion with God's Holy Spirit.

Since the spirit is the source of the spiritual life in man, we may inquire:

Is it possible that the spirit falls, sins and be defiled?

Yes, the spirit may sin the same as the body. It may sin alone without the body, and may sin with the body. It may also lead the body to sin. Let us explain all this in detail because some wrongly think that every wrongdoing is due to the body and the body leads the spirit to fall.

There are many faults in which the spirit may fall alone:

For example, there are the faults in which some angels fell:

The angles are spirits as the psalm says, *"Who makes His angels spirits, His ministers a flame of fire"* (Ps. 104: 4). A group of these angels fell, i.e., the devil, who is described as *"the dragon, that serpent of the old, who is the Devil and Satan"* (Rev. 20:2). St. John the Visionary said that he saw *"war broke out in heaven: Michael and his angels fought against the dragon; and the dragon and his angles fought"* (Rev. 12:7).

Those angels who fell were called the evil or unclean spirits.

The Lord Christ gave His disciples power over unclean spirits to cast them out (Mt. 10: 1). And He said to the seventy disciples whom He sent out, *"Nevertheless, do not rejoice in this, that the spirits are subject to you, but rather rejoice because your names are written in heaven"* (Lk. 10: 20).

The first sin in which Satan fell -though a spirit- is pride.

Pride made Satan say in his heart, *"I will exalt my throne above the stars of God... I will ascend above the heights of the clouds, I will be like the Most High"* (Isa. 14, 13, 14).

Satan -though a spirit- fell also in envy.

We say to the Lord in the Holy Mass [The death which entered into the world through the envy of Satan You destroyed].

Satan envied man because God loved him and made him in His own image and after His likeness. So, Satan made man fall and deserve the condemnation of death.

Satan -though a spirit- fell in lying and tempting others.

Satan lied when he said to Adam and Eve *"You will not surely die"* (Gen. 3: 4). The Lord described him as liar and the father of it" (Jn. 8: 44). He used to cover his lies with tricks by which he tempts the world and still stumbles people and leads them astray. It is said about him that at the end of ages, when he will be released from his prison, he will go out *"to deceive the nations"* (Rev. 20: 8).

Thus, the spirit without the body may fall in pride, envy, lying and tempting others. It is also written about pride:

"**Pride goes before destruction,**

And a haughty spirit before a fall" (Prov. 16: 18).

So, a haughty spirit is a sin in which many people fall as the devil fell.

When the spirit falls in haughtiness, it takes the body with it. So, haughtiness is seen in his looks, his voice, his way of sitting and walking and in his movements. The haughtiness of his spirit is transferred to the body also. Every haughtiness of the spirit can easily attract the body with it.

It is well known that pride and haughtiness emanate from the spirit before the body.

Eve's sin started from the spirit first; her spirit was subjected to the temptation of the serpent. She desired to be like God. At this point, the body began to lust for the prohibited fruit, then to take and eat.

The spirit and the body work together:

The spirit may sin first and the body sins with it, or the body is dominated by the lust and the spirit lusts with it whereas the mind and thinking are involved.

Vice versa, the spirit may be inflamed with righteousness and love of God and attracts the body with it in its spirituality.

The humbleness of the spirit leads to the humbleness of the body.

The spirit's fear and awe of God makes the body bow, kneel on prosterate as we say in the psalm, *"But as for me, I will come into Your house in the multitude of Your mercy. In fear of You I will worship..."* (Ps. 5: 7). The fear of the spirit made the body worship.

The awe dominating over the spirit makes a person take off his shoes before coming into the temple as God said to Moses, when Moses saw the bush burning but not consumed, *"Take your sandals off your feet, for the place where you stand is holy ground"* (Ex. 3: 5). The same words were said to Joshua son of Nun (Josh. 5: 15). If some do enter God's holy sanctuary with their shoes on as in any other place, it is because the spirit is not humbled, nor is the body!

I wonder for those who sometimes pray while sitting!!

Where is the humbleness of spirit and body!!
The body should at least stand before God in awe and respect. Some may ask with which should we begin? With the humbleness of the body or of the spirit? In fact if you start with the humbleness of the spirit, the body will be humbled, and if you start with the humbleness of the body, the spirit will be humbled.

If you are used to bow when you say "Holy, Holy, Holy," this bowing by the body will bring humbleness to your spirit. Likewise, when you take off your shoes before going into the sanctuary, this will make you feel you are in a holy place and will bring humbleness to your spirit.

Fasting and bodily cleanliness before partaking of the Holy Communion will make you feel how awful the Sacrament is. This will make your spirit humble and be prepared spiritually.

Since man is a body and a spirit united together, that which happens to one will happen to the other whether positively or negatively. If the body is careless, the spirit will also be, and according to the carefulness of the body the spirit will be careful.

This does not apply to dealing with God alone but also to our dealings with people also.

If you feel respect within you for someone, this respect will appear in your bowing by the body when greeting him. But if there is haughtiness and carelessness of spirit within you, your body will reflect this when greeting him.

There is an exchanged response between the spirit and the body, unless they are divided.

If the spirit and the body are divided, there will be struggling between them; each will resist the other. A person will live this duplicity until one of two things happens: Either the body submits to the spirit in obedience and walk with it in righteousness, or the spirit submits to the body and walks with it in recklessness.

The spirit is God's image:

When God made man in His own image after His likeness (Gen. 1: 26, 27), it was the spirit that was made in God's image. How was the spirit in God's image?

1. The spirit was in God's image in righteousness and holiness:

In (Eph. 4: 24), St. Paul speaks about the renewal of man and restoration of his original image *"which was created according to God, in righteousness and true holiness."*

When the spirit restores its original image, it restores righteousness and holiness because the human spirit by its nature is good. Evil is new to it.

2. Man is also in God's image in knowledge:

That is why man's spirit is distinguished for reason and utterance. Since the very beginning, God gave Adam knowledge, so he gave names to all the animals *"And whatever Adam called each living creature, that was its name"* (Gen. 2: 19). However, we should be aware that man's knowledge however extensive and growing is limited unlike God's knowledge which is limitless (this point will be expounded in our book: So Many Years With the Problems of People).

3. Man's spirit is in God's image in freedom:

God created man with a free will, and through this free will he fell. God knew that this freedom may make man fall and sin, and that man's salvation would need incarnation and redemption. Yet, God preferred to do this for the sake of providing man with a free spirit to walk in righteousness voluntarily, not be compelled to this.

That is why when God gave His Commandments to the people in the days of Moses the Prophet, God said, *"See, I have set before you today life and good, death and evil... blessing and cursing; therefore choose life, that both you and your descendants may live; that you may love the Lord your God"* (Deut. 30: 15, 19).

See to what extent God loved man that He created him in His own image in freedom though He knew that man will sin and the price of his salvation will be incarnation, pain, disgrace, crucifixion, death and burial.

God preferred this to make man walk in the way of good unvoluntarily. God left man to choose good by his own free will.

Without His freedom, God would have not given the Commandment and the reward or punishment.

4. God created man's spirit in His image in power:

When God created Adam and Eve, He said to them, *"Be fruitful and multiply; fill the earth and subdue it; have dominion over the fish of the sea, over the birds of the air, and over every living thing that moves on the earth"* (Gen. 1:

28). God gave the same blessing of power again to Noah and his children when the ark landed. (Gen. 9: 1,2)

There remains another critical and substantial point in the subject of God's image; which is:

5. Since God has created man in His own image, and God is limitless, to what extent does man have this attribute?

Indeed, God alone is limitless, no one can be like Him in this divine attribute. How can man be in God's image in this point whereas man like any other living creature is limited?
The reply is:

Man is limited but God provided him with the aspiration for the limitless.

His spirit longs to God the limitless and has unlimited aspiration to spiritualities and to the life of perfection.

An example of this is St. Paul the Apostle who ascended to the third heaven (2 Cor. 12: 2, 4) and who labored more abundantly than all the apostles (1 Cor. 15: 10). Yet he said, *"Not that I have already attained, or am already perfected; but I press on... but one thing I do, forgetting those things which are behind and reaching forward to those things which are ahead. I press toward the goal for the prize of the upward call of God in Christ Jesus."* (Phil. 3:12-14)

For what was St. Paul pressing forward?

What did he want to attain more than he had attained? Undoubtedly, it is the aspiration to the limitless.

Thus, there is ambition within everyone's spirit. Ambition may be for pressing forward, for love of ideals, for reaching forward to the limitless, for love of perfection... etc. Yet, everyone directs his aspiration the direction he likes, thus the types of ambition differ but ambition itself exists and is represented in the aspiration for the limitless.

There are still much to be said about the spirit.

❖ ❖ ❖

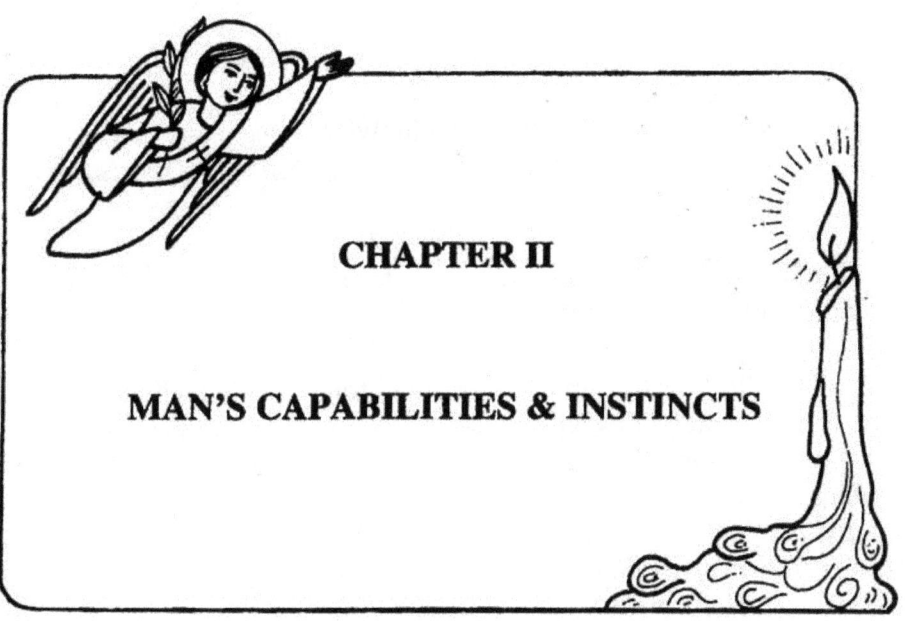

CHAPTER II

MAN'S CAPABILITIES & INSTINCTS

MAN'S CAPABILITIES

God has provided man with many capabilities, each has its functions, strengths and powers; among which are:

The intellect, the spirit, the soul, the conscience, the will, the senses ... etc.

In addition there are the gifts with which God endows every person separately. The level of these capabilities differs from one person to another.

Believe me, we still do not know how great these wonderful human capabilities are.

Who did ever imagine that the mind for example could reach to invent space ships which go to moon directly and man could walk on it! Or imagine that the mind could invent satellites which go around the world, collect news and send pictures of planets! Who did ever imagine that the human mind could invent electronic computers, and employ a machine in quick thinking, in collecting information and in deducing facts.

These capabilities of the mind are not against religion because it is God who created the mind and provided it with such capabilities

Whatever the mind attains is ultimately due to God. - blessed be His name- who provided the mind with all these powers when He created it. We can even say that we have not yet discovered all intellectual capabilities by which we can invent things that do not occur at present to man's mind!

The spirit in man has also wonderful amazing powers.

People do not know all the powers of the spirit, they have not yet discovered them nor utilized them because they did not practise such exercises that activate the spirit and give it the natural strength it has. When we read about the exercises of the spirit practised by some Hindu groups and Yoga and see all the results they attained, we feel astonished. They are not supernatural miracles or powers but natural abilities of the spirit which we do not employ because we neglect them or are not aware of them.

The powers of senses as well are not all utilized. This is due to our being not aware of our need to them. Non-utilization thereof turned to concealed latent powers which appear only when we lose a certain sense and compensate for it by activating other senses instead.

For example a person who loses his sight, tries to compensate for this by the hearing or touching. Thus the hearing or touching gets strengthened and perhaps the smelling also because he trained these senses very well to be means for knowledge instead of the sight. In this way the huge powers of these senses appear though they were not manifest but latent when not utilized.

A perfect person who is perfect in mind, in spirit and in all his senses never existed yet, with the exception of the Lord Christ in His humanity of course.

Man's nature, to be perfect from all aspects needs care and striving so that man does not lose these powers and capabilities. It needs also exercises to protect them so that they might grow.

Certainly, everyone has to develop his powers and capabilities, and to develop also the gifts endowed to him by God.

God gave you intellect and special acuteness or strong memory, but you have not only to maintain all this but also to develop them. You have to improve your ability to think properly, to reach conclusions and solve problems.

The mathematical and geometrical exercises which we studied in school were not just for general knowledge or specialization, but they were useful for training the mind to think properly.

Take for example the chess game between two players; each keeps silent, thinking of the next step the other will take and how he should respond, how the other will respond too, how he will behave then, how he will detain his plans, how he will plan artfully to reach the desired result even after many steps! It is an exercise of intelligence not mere amusement.

Riddles and quizzes also are exercises for the mind.

There are many similar exercises for intelligence and for improving the ability of thinking.

You can use these exercises yourself or for your children and pupils so that they may grow with a powerful intellect trained to think well and when they face a problem, their mind might be ready to face it without being confused.

In practical life there are exercises for wise behavior, or for improving thinking through consulting others and making use of their experiences.

Your conscience as well needs development:

When St. Paul says, *"I have lived in all good conscience before God until this day"* (Acts 23: 1), he is reminding us that there is good conscience and wicked conscience, there is conscience that swallows a camel, and conscience that strains out a gnat and in both the Scribes and Pharisees fell (Mt. 23: 24). There is sick conscience that does not discern well between the good and the evil, and there is weak conscience that is affected by external factors.

Conscience may develop through listening to sermons and spiritual preaching, through sound knowledge and through the effect of good example.

You need to feed your conscience with all this and to get used to judge and blame yourself for all your faults notwithstanding how small they are. At the same time, you have to get used to being serious and strict.

Through all these means your conscience will improve in knowledge, in judgment and in self-control provided that you should avoid suspicions which imagine evil where there is no evil or which enlarge the faults more than they deserve.

Your knowledge also needs to improve

Your knowledge will naturally develop as you grow up in age, but there is also development through providing this natural improvement with proper material. Hence, a person who is keen on improving his knowledge becomes a well-cultured person far from the ignorance fighting the self, and can therefore be a useful member in society and get benefit to himself too.

Knowledge nourishes one's intellect and one's conscience, leading one to sound behavior.

By this one might be able not only to discern between good and evil, but also between what is proper and what is not, helping one to be wise, to behave properly and to deal successfully with others. One may even grow to acquire the ability to give guidance to others.

A person needs also to develop and strengthen his willpower.

Many people know what is good but have no will power to do it, many know what is evil and know its harmful effect but their will power is too weak to foresake it. Their will is unable to resist sin though they know all its consequences; it is because the desire or lust dominates over the will and leads it in its way.

The will is a two-edged weapon that may be used for good or evil.

Everyone needs to sanctify and strengthen his will so that it might be a useful power for his spiritualies. There are many exercises for strengthening the will, among which are the exercises of self control, fasting, control over tongue, senses, thinking and nerves, and exercises for getting rid of bad habits.

Through improving the will we are able to discern between freedom and laxation.

All of us love freedom, but we have to train ourselves to walk in freedom with good will and straight conscience and in spiritual life and attachment to God, otherwise freedom will turn into a kind of laxation and a person loses control over his will and cannot direct his life in a sound way.

Your life, with all its capabilities, is a talent given you from God to take care of.

You have to improve your personality in general so as it becomes a strong straight personality with regard to intellect, conscience, will, knowledge, wisdom and behavior, judging matters or sound disposition.

For all this you need to give due care and to make good use of time.

Many people spend their time in worthless things, in mere entertainment and amusement, or seek means to waste their time without heeding to make use of it in building their personality properly. Those need to be concerned about building themselves by being keen on developing their knowledge and culture, on strengthening their will power, and on attaining by their minds and spirits the most sublime position possible. They have to utilize their capabilities for their own benefit and for the benefit of others besides developing, purifying and strengthening these capabilities.

Do not leave your personality without any control, any care or any improvement.

Do not concentrate on the outward like a girl whose only concern is about here outward appearance, her beauty and her dress! Her only judge is the mirror by which she gets satisfied. She may not use except this mirror for the outward and have no inner mirror by which she can see the condition of the spirit, the mind, the soul and the conscience.

Another person may concentrate only on positions, titles and money, neglecting the interior.

The body also is a power given man by God as a gift.

The body is the executive instrument for all decisions of the spirit, the mind, the will and the conscience. A strong body is able to carry out such decisions, but a weak body cannot.

Body diseases do easily affect the soul.

Diseases cause pain or sadness, distress or complaint. Some people may suffer types of psychological diseases due to body diseases or break down, helplessness and confusion. They may be very concerned about how to deal with the infirmities of their bodies.

There are certain body diseases which have a deep effect on the capabilities of the body such as cerebral concussion or bleeding of the brain which may affect some brain functions as memory, movement or voice; and arteriosclerosis which may lead to amnesia. The body nerves affect one's mood and behavior, and heart diseases affect one's capabilities.

The body lusts have their impact on the mind and conscience.

The lusts try to use the mind in realizing its desires and try to silence the conscience or try to find execuses and justification for the desires!!

The body lust may dominate completely over the intellect to achieve its desires, and may also weaken the spirit and cut its relationship with God.

Hence we should give due care to our bodies; not to let them weaken to the extent of affecting our capabilities, nor excite our instincts lest they should weaken our spirits.

An important point noteworthy in this regard, is:

Maintaining balance, co-operation and integrity among the capabilities of the person.

There should be no contradiction or conflict among one's capabilities. Any division or inner conflict should be avoided.

Some author, describing the conflict between his feelings and his conscience, said [I was fighting and struggling with myself as if I were two persons in one; one pushing and the other preventing me].

How easy it is for one's capabilities to fight: *"the flesh lusts against the spirit, and the spirit against the flesh"* (Gal. 5: 17); or the soul against the conscience or the intellect against the will.

A person may find himself divided as if he were two fighting together! Different ways pulling him, he falls in conflict between his love of good and his lust for sin or between thoughts which he cannot discern whether they are good or not as the poet Ilia Abu Madi says in his poem "I know not":

> Behold! Is it a fight or conflict within?
> Sometimes I seem a devil, other times an angel within!
> Am I two in one, between them participation is not;
> Or am I imagining things? I know not.

A straight sound personality has no such conflict.

There may be conflict between the person and external factors or wars whereas he is stable within and undivided with regard to his feelings and will. He is one, fighting with all his powers an external war.

An internal war may happen because one power in a person wishes to dominate over the other powers or over some of them.

A person may for example have control over his intellect and he behaves well. But some lust or agitation may prevail and the intellect deviates and is subjected to it. That is why we often say:

It is so easy for the intellect to be a servant obedient to the soul's desires!

The soul may have a sinful desire which it insists on and submits to subjecting the mind to it introduce evidences to support it using if necessary Verses from the Holy bible and giving them appropriate interpretation or using tales from the holy fathers. Moreover, if the soul desires the opposite, the mind will provide it with evidences supporting it.

For instance a child does wrong, and his mother with her mind defends him in response to the heart feelings, whereas the same wrongdoing is done by another child and the same mother criticizes him severely because her heart did not persuade her to defend him.

The mind sometimes -as we have seen- weighs with two different scales.

The cause of such contradiction is that the mind was free in one case and submitting to the soul in the other. A just man having a free intellect judges correctly the right thing even though it may be done by his enemy and the wrong thing as false though it may be done by his father or brother.

The mind submits to many impacts

ORIENTED CAPABILITIES, INSTINCTS AND GIFTS

God created man with many natural capabilities including instincts, some of which seem destructive or misused. However, everything in man's nature can be used for good, even that which some think to be evil. The following are some examples we give:

Obstinacy:

A person may fall in the hands of a severe guide who destroys his capabilities and inner life, whereas a wise guide directs his capabilities to good.

Let us apply this to obstinacy, for example:
Is obstinacy considered a sin or a capability?
Is it originally a capability which deviated into a sin?

In fact obstinacy is a sin if it is related to a wrongdoing. But when it is used for good, it is called persistence, steadfastness and holding to good.

* Take for example the stories of the heroes of faith:

St. Athanasius the apostolic was a very obstinate adversary to the Arians. He defended sound faith in a rare firmness and iron will against Arius and the Arians who were in their utmost strength and power. He was condemned more than once and exiled four times. When they said to him "The world is against you, Athanasius", he said, "and I am against the world".

The matter turns to persistence, firmness and steadfastness without any slackening or leniency so long as one is on the right path.

* The same may be said with regard to the martyrs and confessors.

They had amazing steadfastness in faith in spite of all temptations, threats, imprisonment, exile and terrible torturing. Their hearts were firm and unshaking, a matter which made their persecutors describe them as obstinate and stubborn. But it was holy obstinacy or steadfastness in faith.

* **With the same firmness monks join monasticism.**

A person resists himself when the world tries to tempt him with all means and struggles against all thoughts of the enemy disregarding them. He may be resisted even by his parents and family who influence him with various emotions and hard pressures which sometimes are severe! But the person seeking monasticism remains firm and does not deviate.

* **The same goes with those who seek any type of consecration**

They are fought by various means but they face such wars with steadfast heart, firm mind and strong will. They do not move or shake. Some may call this stubbornness, but it is in fact persistence

* **There is also resistance against oneself during spiritual struggles.**

One should resist oneself in fasting, in chastity, in guarding one's thoughts and senses, in controlling one's tongue and nerves and in any spiritual exercises. It is called the virtue of forcing oneself. There should be resistance in all spiritual wars and resistance against sin as St. Paul the Apostle says rebuking those who slacken, *"You have not yet resisted to bloodshed striving against sin"* (Heb. 12: 4)

All this needs stubbornness in fighting against the devil, the sin and the body

In this way, the devil will find himself before a powerful person uneasy to shake or bend; if he tries to go into his heart and mind, he will find him *"A garden enclosed ... a spring shut up, a fountain sealed"* (Song 4: 12). The man of God stands against the devil resisting in persistence as a hard rock that does not soften ...

Why then do people look to stubborness as a bad thing?

* The bad stubborness is persistence in the offense.

In such a case, a person walks in the wrong way and refuses any understanding or honest advice with a closed mind resisting any reformation even though the advice is given by a faithful friend, a spiritual father or a trustworthy guide, and even though the right is evident.

In this case, it is mere stubborness of mind and will, not steadfastness in the right

We should with discernment and wisdom differentiate between the two matters and not mix up between them! We should observe this very well in breeding the young, in bringing up children and in guiding youth.

If there is stubborness arising from a strong will, we should direct it towards good.

A strong firm will should be kept and not destroyed but rather be directed towards good with the same power so that it might be of benefit for the person, that he might not sin and for others.

Anger:

Anger is a power even though it is sinful.

* Anger may be considered a sin if it is fleshly and psychic

It will be fleshly if it turns into nervousness and rage accompanied by high voice, violence, and uncontrolled features and movements with harshness and hard words.

It is psychic when involving wrath and hatred, self-avenging, raging of the heart and mind in an unspiritual way, and may even be worse involving insults, hurting of feeling or beating.

* However, anger is a power that can be used for good

As explained in our book on "Anger", it may be sometimes holy anger ... as Moses the Prophet, who was said to be *"very humble more than all men who were on the face of the earth"*

(Num. 12: 3), when he saw the people worshipping the golden calf his anger became hot, he took the calf which they had made, burned it in the fire, ground it to powder and scattered it, then he rebuked Aaron the high priest (Ex. 32: 19-21)

So, anger -as a power- may be directed to good

John Cassian wrote a chapter on "Anger" in his book "The Institutes" in which he stated the sayings of the fathers on the verse, *"Be angry, and do not sin"* (Ps. 4: 4). He said,

Your anger will not be sin if you are angry for your sins

A person will not be sinning if he is angry for his sins, weakness or falls. This holy anger may lead him to avoid sinning in the future. In this case, he would have directed his power of anger the right way against himself to rectify himself not against others

Does this not conform with the words of the Lord, *"And if your right eye causes you to sin, pluck it out and cast it from you."* (Mt. 5: 29).

In fact we do not destroy the power of anger but we direct it well.

The power of anger can produce enthusiasm, holy zeal and energy. But if destroyed, a person becomes sluggish.

With the power of anger a person resists evil as Phinehas the priest did and God praised and rewarded him (Num. 25: 6-13).

David also, getting angry, resisted Goliath and saved the people from his arrogance and defiance (1 Sam. 17: 26-51).

A spiritual person cannot see the evil and his heart does not move within him! When St. Paul the Apostle went to Athens, *"his spirit was provoked within him when he saw that the city was given over to idols"* (Acts 17: 16).

However, if a person gets angry for a spiritual purpose, his wrath should be in a spiritual way.

A spiritual purpose should be achieved through spiritual means. A person in this case should not insult, be proud or haughty, behave unseemly or lose control over his tongue or pen in a way lacking good manners and decency!!

As the purpose is directed to be holy, the means also should be directed to be holy.

Ambition:

Ambition is not a sin, but rather a holy power, by which a person aspires to perfection in God's image.

God has created us in His own image, after His likeness (Gen. 1: 26). God, being limitless, has put in us the longing for the limitless; He said to us, *"Therefore you shall be perfect, just as your Father in heaven is perfect"* (Mt. 5: 48).

Ambition may be directed in a spiritual way.

St. Paul the Apostle who was caught up to the third heaven (2 Cor. 12: 2-4) and who labored more abundantly than all the apostles (1 Cor. 15: 10), says, *"Brethren, I do not count myself to have apprehended; but one thing I do, forgetting those things which are behind and reaching forward to those things which are ahead, I press toward the goal ... "* (Phil. 3: 13).

This reaching forward is due to the spiritual ambition.

Spiritual ambition thus leads to spiritual growth and involves one's whole life

Ambition involves everything a person does, whether in his studies, his job or his family and worldly responsibilities as St. John the Beloved said, *"I pray that you may prosper in all things and be in health, just as your soul prospers"* (3 Jn. 2) ... in all things ... as the psalm says about a blessed man that, *"whatever he does shall prosper"* (Ps. 1: 3). The same was said about Joseph the Righteous in (Gen. 39: 3).

Spiritual ambition does not mean to surpass others but to surpass objectively

It means that you do the work with an ideal perfectness, not just surpass others. At the same time you ought to wish that all your competitors do the work with the same ideal perfectness. Ambition should not make you lose your love to the people.

It is spiritual ambition that involves continual spiritual growth in every virtue. It is ambition in all your works and responsibilities that you may attain every possible perfection without being detained by any personal inclination.

Ambition should not take a materialistic or worldly trend.

An example of this trend is ambition for wealth, titles, positions, authority, love of the world or pride of life.

Power:

God's children should be powerful because they are the image of God Almighty, but power should take a spiritual trend.

How beautiful the words of the Lord are, *"But you shall receive power when the Holy Spirit has come upon you; and you shall be witnesses to Me ..."* (Acts 1: 8)! It is written also, *"And with great power the apostles gave witness to the resurrection of the Lord Jesus. And great grace was upon them all"* (Acts 4: 33).

When one of your children wishes to be powerful, do not destroy this wish within him ...

You ought to direct such wish the right way that he might be spiritually powerful with power of will and power in overcoming sin, power in serving, in convincing others, in knowledge, in love, in sacrifice & in impact on others and that he might be powerful in his spiritual exercises, in his prayers and in his contemplations.

In such way the power will not be like that of Samson or worldly power.

Power does not mean overcoming others, but rather winning them.

Self-Love:

Is loving oneself a sin?

No, for the Holy Bible says, *"You shall love your neighbor as yourself"* (Mt. 22: 39).

The important thing is that your self-love takes a spiritual attitude.

Thus you love for yourself to attain purity and holiness, to be a holy temple for the Holy Spirit and to attain a share in the Kingdom, being blameless before God and victorious, joining those who overcame and won, and to be lead in triumph in Christ (2 Cor. 2: 14).

Let not your love for yourself make you fall into indulgence.

Nor let you say as Solomon had said, *"Whatever my eyes desired I did not keep from them"* (Eccl. 2: 10).

True love of oneself is manifested in certain well known virtues including self-control, self-examining and self blaming or rebuking for sins.

True love of oneself contradicts with selfishness and favoring oneself rather than others.

The Lord says, "*And whoever exalts himself will be abased, and he who humbles himself will be exalted*" (Mt. 23: 12). It is also written, " ... *in honor giving preference to one another*" (Rom. 12: 10).

Do you love yourself? That is good. With this love improve yourself to restore the image of God, and beware not to love yourself in a wrong way!

If you do love your self, bring it to the cross so that when it suffers with Him, it may also be glorified (Rom. 8: 17), so that it may be able to sing, "*I have been crucified with Christ; it is no longer I who live, but Christ lives in me*" (Gal. 2: 20).

If you do love your self, lead it to self-denial so that it may be like the Lord Christ who made Himself of no reputation (Phil. 2: 7).

It is not love that you pamper yourself but you are rather destroying yourself, whereas the Lord required the opposite when He said, "*He who finds his life will lose it, and he who loses his life for My sake will find it*" (Mt. 10: 39).

Gifts:

Suppose someone has the gift of drawing, carving, poetry, music, creating tunes, or even the gift of acting, singing or alike matters ... would we restrain such a gift and direct him to a spiritual path under the pretext that such a gift leads him away from God !!

Nay, we should direct all such gifts to be used spiritually.

We do need all these gifts for the church, we need some people to write songs, some others who are clever in music to compile tunes for the songs, others who have gifted voices and who have the ability to play music to form choirs.

We even need to establish a Coptic theatre

Such a theatre will produce beautiful plays presenting the history of martyrs, father monks and saints in an effective way. These plays can be recorded as films or video tapes to be watched by youth and families and presented in villages in rural service.

All these require the talent of writing, acting, prompting, producing or make up and photography. Study of the dresses fashion of every age and the ability of making them are also required. Nothing is wrong in all this.

The only wrong thing is misusing the gift.

On the other hand, it is useful and beneficial to use the gift in a spiritual way to offer a successful service and to attract our children away from confusing films to other films filling them with spiritual feelings. All this is useful and of great benefit, not at all wrong, but rather failure to do this would be wrong.

Nothing is wrong in arts, but deviation thereof is wrong.

We should thus fight deviation not art, and should not restrain gifts, remembering in all this the words of the apostle, *"To the pure all things are pure, but to those who are defiled and unbelieving nothing is pure"* (Tit. 1: 15).

To the pure all things are pure:
We should use every gift and every attribute in purity.

Should we use arts with purity, it will be pure also.
Should we use anger with purity, it will turn into spiritual enthusiasm and holy zeal. Even drugs, when used in surgical operations it turns pure in this medical field for those who are pure.

Fear might be a defect and may turn into a psychological disease, but if we direct it towards God's fear it becomes pure for those who are pure. In this way, fear turns into a virtue giving protection from falling into sin.

Intelligence is also pure for the pure, but to those who are not pure it turns into a destructive power, into subtlety, intrigue and plotting ...

Love may be pure for the pure and is distinguished for faithfulness, giving, honesty and sacrifice, but to the impure it may turn into impurity, fondling or destructive selfishness ...

Everything is judged according to its use, its aim and its means.

With the spiritual aim and good means we can turn all powers to good, to building people and to building the kingdom.

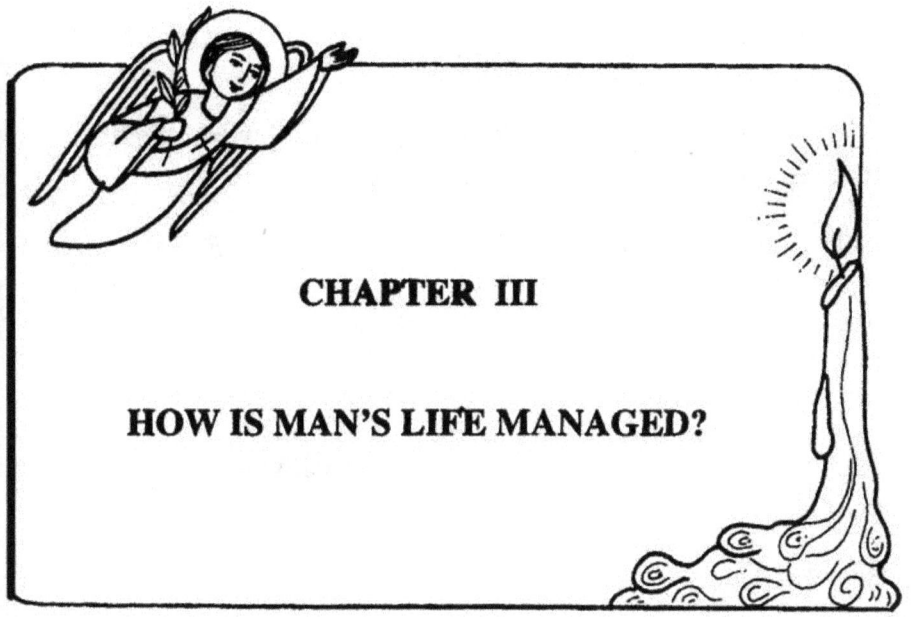

CHAPTER III

HOW IS MAN'S LIFE MANAGED?

HOW IS MAN'S LIFE MANAGED?

Man's behavior is controlled by many powers among which are the intellect, the spirit, the flesh, the soul, the conscience, the nerves, the gifts, the powers and capabilities.

In an even person, all powers should work together without contradiction or conflict.

It is true that the epistle to the Galatians says, *"For the flesh lusts against the spirit, and the spirit against the flesh; and these are contrary to one another, so that you do not do the things that you wish"* (Gal 5: 17), but by these words is meant the spiritual person who is a beginner in striving. When such a person overcomes in his striving, there will be no fighting between his flesh and his spirit, but both will work together for God.

The Intellect:

Some may say that man is lead by his intellect, but...

The intellect is not the only guide for man.

Man might be led by psychological, nervous or emotional factors. He might be also led by his own conscience. His mind might be thinking in one way and his conscience in another.

Man might be led by his temper and attitudes.

Such temper might be deep rooted from childhood and does not change. So, a person might confess, partake, pray, fast, read and contemplate whereas his temper remains as it is or might be led by certain habits prevailing in spite of his thinking or conscience.

The mind might sometimes err in the advice it gives and in judging matters, and the conscience might also err, for the Holy Bible says,

"There is a way which seems right to a man, but its end is the way of death" (Prov. 14: 12).

As this saying is important, it is repeated in (Prov. 16: 25).

Of course, this destructive way leading to death is certainly approved by the mind and the conscience because it seems right to a man.

If we say that man should follow the mind, what mind it should be? The mind should be healthy; for there are kinds of intellect.

The mind must sometimes be an obedient servant to the desires of the soul.

In such a case when the soul wants something, the mind will provide it with evidences and proofs, and even with evidences from the Holy Bible but interpreted in a way satisfying the soul and the conscience as well. It is easy for the mind to give sayings of the fathers which were said on a certain occasion and cuts them off forming them in a way acceptable to the soul. The mind goes with the soul wherever it goes either in its anger or its contentment! Hence, man's mind needs to be instructed.

The minds of some people might cause them trouble, while other minds give comfort.

Someone might be troubled because of his mind which provides him with suspicions, doubts and thoughts or fears, or because his mind does not think in a sound way or make account for the consequences of the thoughts. This mind might be like a whirlpool, when the person goes into it he drowns and is swallowed.

The mind might also be the cause of trouble if it is by its nature pessimistic or apprehensive, predicts harm where there is no harm and thinks of perdition, death or dark future without a justifiable cause.

Some minds magnify problems.

Such a mind gives problems a size bigger than the natural one, imagining danger, or mixing up matters, connecting events together in a way complicating everything and creating bad relations! Such a mind might bring forth events that had passed a long time ago adding to them apprehensions from unknown future thus pressing on one's soul with this way of thinking.

A person may be troubled by a persecution complex in his mind which makes him imagine that all people around him do not love him. For example, a girl imagines that her parents love her sister more than her...

A person may be troubled because his mind is attached to imagination.

The imagination might be sinful, by which a person imagines forms of sin satisfying himself with them, or creates dreamy imagination, which may be called "day dreams," by which he lives hopes and wishes far from actuality. He is satisfied with such imagination and feels pleased with it thus wasting his time without working for it! Such wishes might be for titles, positions, wealth... etc.

A person's mind might block the way before him.

He might think sometimes that there is no salvation (Ps. 3). His mind might lead him to commit suicide as a result of despair and inability to reach a solution and because the mind refuses to reveal the problems to the guides that they may find solutions for them.

Unlike this type is a person whose mind gives him comfort.

A mind of this kind solves the problems of the person in a sound way tactfully and wisely, and even help him solve the problems of the others.

Even philosophers! The startpoint with some of them might be subject to various influences!

The philosophy of some philosophers might not be purely intellectual, but affected by some family, social, economic or political factors which formed their minds in a certain way on which they built their philosophy.

In most cases the mind is rarely pure intellect.

The mind does not work alone, but many factors interfere with it.

Among these factors are: traditions, environment and inherited habits.

Traditions:

Traditions force the mind to do certain acts such as giving the elder daughter in marriage before her sisters even though good suitors come. The father refuses them without a reasonable cause except for traditions. Laban did so when he gave Leah in marriage before Rachel (Gen. 29: 22-27). His conscience and mind forced him to do so even though with fraud and deceit!!

In most cases the younger sister is the victim of her father's subjection to tradition especially if she is more beautiful than the elder.

Furthermore, people spend much money due to traditions used in engagement and marriage ceremonies or even in funerals, or feasts... etc. The mind might advice differently but cannot do because it is subject to traditions.

That is why it is written, *"Lean not on your own understanding"* (Prov. 3: 5).

Therefore, God gave spiritual guides and leaders. The mind has become in need to be subject to guidance.

Guidance:

It might be impossible for man to be led absolutely be his own understanding or even by his own conscience, each being deficient, or because he tries to form his mind and conscience in a way that satisfies him.

He needs another mind beside his own that is not subject to psychological influences. He needs a good conscience beside his own if the latter is not just in judging. It is true:

Those who have no guide fall like the leaves of trees.

Guidance is necessary to save a person from being subject with his mind to his own desires!

The mind and the desires cooperate together yielding for one another and supporting each other to attain what they want.

Man is often led by his nerves:

Nerves:

Nerves are not mere organic function but the psychological factor often accompany them. When one is psychologically in trouble, the nerves will be inflamed, and when one is nervously inflamed, he suffers psychological troubles. Each trouble becomes a cause and a result to the other.

When nerves get inflamed, they might take the lead and stop all powers of the mind and conscience dominating alone.

In such a case one's behavior becomes random without self-control.

Then the spirit -if allowed- will interfere as an ointment calming the nerves down and leading the mind in the right way. So, the person calms down and the conscience wakes up and rebukes the person for his previous random behavior.

The Conscience:

What conscience is that which should lead man?

The Holy Bible mentions a special attribute for conscience, i.e. good conscience (Acts 23: 1), (1 Tim. 1: 5, 19), (Heb. 13: 18).

There might be bad conscience, therefore it was right that St. Paul the Apostle said the beautiful words, *"I myself always strive to have a conscience without offense toward God and men"* (Acts 24: 16).

There is a wide conscience that swallows a camel and a narrow suspicious conscience that strains out a gnat (Mt. 23: 24) like that of the scribes and Pharisees.

On the other hand, a good conscience is like the scale that weighs gold in its accuracy when judging any matter, or like the scale of the Pharmacist which harms if not accurate whether indicating higher or lower weight.

A good conscience is enlightened by the guidance of the Holy Spirit

Such a conscience does not give its own guidance depending on mere human knowledge, but is guided by God's Spirit and obeys God's good word and divine teaching.

Sometimes, man is led by his emotions not by his nerves:

The Emotions:

Most people are led by their emotions and feelings whether love or hatred, envy or jealously, sacrifice or giving. Women are perhaps led by their emotions more than men.

But emotions alone are not sufficient; they should be mixed with reasoning and wisdom.

Emotions without reasoning are not sufficient, and reasoning without emotions is not sufficient; both perfect each other. That is why God gave the family a father and a mother to perfect each other. Emotions alone may lead to pamper the children, whereas firmness alone may lead to harshness. But when emotions are mixed with firmness they will realize perfection of breeding and balanced treatment.

Balance:

A straight person makes balance between his feelings and emotions, and his actions; balance between reasoning and emotions; and balance between the self and the others.

If a person thinks only of himself without taking others into account, this may lead him to a kind of selfishness and may fail as a social person. If he thinks only of others, he may get tired, becomes bored and grumbles if his sacrificing is not accompanied with great love that makes him forget himself absolutely or makes him concentrate on his eternity not on his life on earth.

A straight person divides his emotions in a straight way.

Such a person makes balance between gay and gloominess in his life, between seriousness and simplicity and between work and amusement, putting before him the words, *"To everything there is a season, a time for every purpose under heaven ... a time to weep, and a time to laugh ... a time to keep silence, and a time to speak ... a time of war, and a time of peace"* (Eccl. 3: 1-8).

A straight person makes balance in dividing his time.

He gives time to work and time to rest, time to bodily needs and time to spiritualities, time to family responsibilities and time to service requirements, time to his mind and to getting knowledge, time to worship and time to social work.

Every responsibility on his shoulders takes the time it needs.

He makes balance between giving and refraining, between taking and giving.

He makes balance between his various emotions.

Other people are led by knowledge:

Knowledge:

They are led by books and other printed material. But this depends on the kind of books or material from which they take their information. Those might take their knowledge also from various mass media.

As knowledge is important in man's life, sinners are called fools.

In the Parable of the Virgins, it is said *"Now five of them were wise, and five were foolish"* (Mt. 25: 2).

And about the atheists it is said, *"The fool has said in his heart, there is no God"* (Ps. 14: 1).

Such a person described in the Holy Bible as fool might be a philosopher!

A fool or an ignorant person is not aware of God's presence and holiness, is not aware of what he himself is doing and its consequences and effect on his eternity. He might also be ignorant of his own nature and of the wars he is facing. He is not aware or feigns unawareness that God sees whatever he does or says. For all this God said,

"*My people are destroyed for lack of knowledge*" (Hos. 4: 6).

The remedy for this is sound knowledge, since wrong knowledge is harmful.

Divine leadership:

The divine leadership is the ideal thing; for the Holy Bible say, "*For as many as are led by the Spirit of God, these are sons of God*" (Rom. 8: 14).

Their spirits are led by God's Spirit, and their bodies and minds are led by their spirits.

God is all in all in their lives.

CHAPTER IV

THE MIND

SINCE THE MIND LEADS MAN, WHAT LEADS THE MIND?

It is well known that man is a rational being, but I argue: To what extent is man rational?

Is man pure intellect? Or is he subject to many influences that make his actions sometimes not perfectly rational?

Here we shall present and examine each of these influences:

1. The first point to discuss here is the type of the mind:

Is it an intelligent mind? a genius? of moderate intelligence? of weak intelligence? or not intelligent at all?

People are of different mentalities with regard to their type and degree of intelligence. According to such difference of understanding, thinking and inference differ.

The type of memory also differs whether be it merely collecting and keeping, or keeping and arranging, or be it photographic memory, whether it helps the person or fails him sometimes.

Of what kind is his thinking? Is it general? Is it concentrated in one side neglecting the others? Is it shallow or deep thinking? How deep is it?

In the same way, to what extent can we say that a person is rational?

People are not equal even in their understanding to what is happening or what should happen. Some people hardly lead themselves, other people can lead others, or need to be lead by others.

2. Some people are troubled by their way of thinking and may trouble others also.

Some people -when facing a problem- can find a solution for it in their mind, but others are absorbed completely by the problem. It may take all their mind and their thinking. It is prevailing when one is awake or asleep, and even in one's dreams. The problem does not leave any chance for a person to think of something else. This of course troubles him and certainly affects his nerves and mood.

3. Some people are dominated by doubt:

Their minds doubt any events and any occurences, doubt people and doubt their acts and intentions, doubt whatever they hear and whatever is said, doubt their own ability to act and doubt what future may bring.

Such people are in trouble and pain because of doubt. Doubt may cause them fear and confusion but their minds are unable to go beyond the circle of doubt! They even doubt any justifications made to remove such doubt, they suspect the truth and the aim of such justifications ...

Doubt might grow with this type of people and extend to everything even to the dearest people, thus they become a prey to rumours, suspicions and lies.

The most serious doubts that dominate over some minds are doubts related to faith.

Example of such doubts are doubts of atheists concerning God's existence, doubts of scientists concerning miracles, doubts concerning the next life and resurrection of bodies and doubts concerning holy scriptures or certain facts and truths of faith and beliefs.

If the mind goes to this extent of doubt, how easy it will be for the devil to make of it a plaything.

In such a case, the opponent will provide him with so many thoughts and guide him to certain readings that may increase his doubts or to companions of the same type who may develop and increase the thoughts fighting him.

Do you think that such a mind is pure intellect though it is led by others?!

4. The mind is affected by ignorance:

Whether ignorance due to lack of knowledge or to false knowledge received by the mind, this makes the person behave in a wrong way. And being unaware of the facts of any subject or any event makes a person subject to suspicions and thoughts which may easily trouble him.

Such a mind needs true convincing knowledge, sound instruction and sometimes needs rebuking with love and good intent to reveal facts.

The most serious ignorance that fights the mind is that which rejects knowledge.

It means that the mind insists on being ignorant, convinced with whatever thoughts it has and doubts any instruction or explanation given. Such a mind might be instructed by temptations or visited by grace to be renewed (Rom. 12: 2). In general as far as a person grows in knowledge, his way of thinking changes according to the kind of knowledge he gets.

5. The minds of some people are led by a certain principle in which they believe:

Such a person lives within this principle whether it is right or wrong. He does not like to move away from such a principle but is locked within it to the extent that it forms a main structure of his life.

Believe me even most of the philosophers who are supposed to be governed by the mind are subject to the saying that the start point of philosophy might sometimes be not philosophical. In other words, they might start with a certain physchological element on which they build their philosophy.

This resembles a ball thrown down from a mountain; if you throw it to the east it will continue with all its strength that direction, and if to the west it will continue so.

6. Another type of mind is led by a father or an instructor:

Such a mind is subject to another mind that leads it as it wishes whether it is the mind of a natural father, a spiritual father, an instructor or a guide.

The person does not let his mind behave or even think away from the circle of such an instructor and his thoughts and guidance. His personality is almost lost especially if the father or guide is authoritative and requires complete passive obedience.

This complete subjection of the mind increases if the person has complete confidence in the person obeyed or if it believes that he will be lost if he disobeys or if he is convinced that mere discussing or arguing with the guide is a kind of pride.

Such a mind does not work; it only obeys another mind.

7. Such a mind might also be led by news or rumours:

It might be led by a book read or a movie, a television or video film, because the mind has got used to obey and to be subject to another effective leadership, be it press news, information heard from people or any person more powerful intellectually than him.

The rumours or information may prove false afterwards but after leaving within him an influence not to be easily removed.

A sane powerful mind, on the other hand, examines and scrutinizes.

It examines and analyzes whatever it hears, and accepts what is convincing refusing anything else or leaving some information for further study and inquiry. It might benefit from what people say but does not obey them completely like a parrot "his mind in his ears."

Some leaders are easily led astray by false reports especially if they are greatly affected by them to the extent that they take hasty decisions based on falsehood.

Many families were dissolved when they believed everything heard.

8. The mind might sometimes be led by the nerves:

This is the case if the mind is quickly affected, quickly agitated and thinks according to its emotions. Samson obeyed Delilah because her persistence pressed on his nerves and his nerves in annoyment and despair forced his mind to reveal his secret.

9. The mind is often subject to family or social influences:

A stepmother often influences the mind of the father making him treat badly his son from his first wife believing whatever things she pours in his ears.

The community also often has its influence on the minds of the people. The individual is thus influenced by the views and reactions of the community, like a pupil taking part in a demonstration repeating the words of those leading such demonstration. When this pupil is arrested and imprisoned, sitting alone his mind begins to think differently and he may blame himself for his rashness following such demonstration.

10. Another factor is called by some people "brain washing":

Here the mind is under successive influences, various doubts and intellectual pressures pulling out what is within and filling the mind with a new thought. The person comes out of this circle in which his mind is locked up to find himself thinking in a new different way. He might even feel zealous for the new thought without giving an opportunity to the other thought to make balance with the pressures on his mind.

11. The mind might be affected by other sects and denominations:

A person might mix, for sometime, with some communists who would turn his mind into communism; or with Jehovah Witnesses, and he becomes a follower and advocate for them. We read about some people who mixed with existentialists, Hibiz, beetles or other sects who left their influence on their minds and they began to think in a different way.

Who mixes with stern people becomes stern, and who mixes with the careless becomes like them. The mind is narrow or indulgent according to the influence.

12. The mind might be affected by the nature of its disposition:

A person of delicate sensitive disposition is easily affected by any word said to him and his mind imagines that it is a serious and hard word, whereas a simple person might accept by his mind matters which no deep thinking person can believe.

13. The mind might be affected by its habits and its nature:

The mind might be led by a habit or nature in matters unacceptable to any wise person. Moreover, the mind might justify such habits or such a nature and justify the behavior resulting therefrom. The mind might perhaps be sure that such a habit is harmful yet it overcomes because the mind is not taking the lead, and as the saying goes "one's nature prevails."

Can we say after all this that man is a rational creature lead by the mind? Certainly not.

14. Another type of mind is led by fear:

Fear paralyzes such a mind making it unable to think and is led by such fear.

Our father Adam, for example, felt afraid and hid behind the tree although reasonably God would certainly see him wherever he goes. He was led by fear not by reason.

Fear might lead the mind to work for it.

When a person does something wrong and is afraid of the results, his mind might make him cover his fault with trickery, lies or false accusation against someone else.

A frightened person cannot be reasonable in his thinking.

15. Some minds might be led by lust:

Whatever this lust might be; lust of the body, lust of revenge, lust of positions or titles, lust of money or lust of greatness... etc., it prevails, and the mind might be led astray as it attempts to satisfy such lust.

A person who is led by the lust of revenge, all his mind is concentrated on how to take revenge without thinking at all of the results nor of God's commandments. He is imprisoned within this lust which prevails alone over his mind. He obeys it and he is lost because his mind does not prevent him from committing crime.

16. The mind might be led by emotion:

Some emotions might lead the mind, and some emotions might be unreasonable. There might also be a mind without emotions and a wise mind having emotions under its control. There are four types, each differs from the other.

The mind led by emotions is like the mother who interferes with her married daughter's affairs led by her emotions alone without reasoning, and the result is the destruction of her daughter's life and marriage.

A pupil, for example, might be led by his emotions and dictates the answers to his friend in the exams, thus he is condemned and punished. The exam might be cancelled for both of them.

Jezebel, in the name of emotions, thought of some means to satisfy her husband and enable him to take possession of the vineyard of Naboth the Jezreelite. She caused his and her own perdition. Her mind caused her to drown in an obyss of religious and human faults.

17. The mind might be led by the Holy Spirit:

The mind might be capable of thinking, but when enlightened by the Holy Spirit. -who gives it the knowledge of all the right- all its thoughts would be completely proper, spiritual and in conformity with God's will.

The most dangerous mind is that which declares its independence from God.

Such a mind behaves according to its human understanding whereas the scriptures say, *"Do not be wise in your own eyes"* (Prov. 3:7), and also, *"lean not on your own understanding"* (Prov. 3:5). On the other hand, one who is led by God's Spirit says *"let Your will be done."*

18. Such a spiritual mind resembles that which is led by God's commandments:

David the Prophet said, *"The commandment of the Lord is pure, enlightening the eyes"* (Ps. 19:8), and, *"Your word is a lamp to my feet and a light to my path"* (Ps. 119:105).

The last two types of mind are led by the Spirit and by good conscience before God, and are also enlightened with the Holy Spirit.

RENEWING OF THE MIND

The mind might err and might be affected by certain factors which make it lose proper sight. Therefore let us contemplate on the words of St. Paul the Apostle in the Epistle to the Romans, *"... be transformed by the renewing of your mind"* (Rom. 12:2).

The importance of renewal:

In baptism our nature is renewed, but the renewal of the mind and of the life style is continually required throughout our lives. One should not be stone frozen in one situation.

The renewal of the mind means change of the look to things.

The term "renewal" is often mentioned in the Psalms and the scriptures. In every prayer of the hours we pray Psalm 51 *"Create in me a clean heart, O God, and renew a steadfast spirit within me."* And in the Nineth Hour Prayer we praise the Lord, saying, *"Oh, sing to the Lord a new song!"* (Ps. 98:1).

Our new form in Christianity is expressed in the words, *"... you have put off the old man with his deeds, and have put on the new man who is renewed in knowledge according to the image of Him who created him"* (Col. 3:9,10). Notice here the words "new" and "renewed" and how it is renewal in knowledge. So, renewal of the mind means that it takes new knowledge which it had not had before.

Such renewal in knowledge is accompanied by a new power for action as the scriptures say, *"Those who wait on the Lord shall renew their strength, they shall mount up with wings like eagles, they shall run and not be weary, they shall walk and not faint"* (Isa. 40:31).

God wants us to have this newness of life; that is why He said in the Book of Ezekiel the Prophet, *"I will give you a new heart and put a new spirit within you"* (Ezek. 36:26).

What then is renewal of the mind?

A person sins because his mind leads him to sin. Therefore, God wants him to have a different look to things.

Take for example one's look to the body.

How a person thinks of the body? Does he consider it a means of enjoyment and pleasure (be it enjoyment of eating, drinking, and clothing or of sexual acts or adultry, or of feeling the beauty or strength of the body)? If this is the case, he will sin.

Here the apostle advises him to renew his mind or in other words that his thinking takes a new form.

Being renewed, one looks to the body as God's temple:

It is God's temple because it is the temple of the Holy Spirit who is in us (1 Cor. 6:19). If the mind is renewed, it will look to the body as mere container of the human spirit or of God's Spirit dwelling in it. Thus with the body one can glorify God as the apostle said, *"... therefore, glorify God in your body and in your spirit, which are God's"* (1 Cor. 6:20).

One should always glorify God in the body and with the body. This can be realized if the body is walking the same way with the spirit. But if the body and the spirit are contrary to one another (Gal. 5:17), it means that the person still lives with the old concept that the body is a means of enjoyment, and he should change his thought in this regard.

Having this concept, even if a person overcomes the lust of the body, he will refrain from sinning but its love will continue within him. But when the mind is renewed, the person will overcome sin because he has become above this level and does not need much effort to get rid of it.

When the mind is renewed, a person will not only look to his body in such a way but also to the bodies of the others. When he looks at a woman he will not lust for her in his heart (Mt. 5:28) because, according to his spiritual understanding, she is a temple of the Holy Spirit, thus she is holy especially when partaking of the Holy Communion.

With his renewed mind, a person looks at a woman as God's daughter, who should be respected far from any uncleanliness and corruption. The woman does not need to cover herself from head to toes so that man may be safe from the lust in his heart. Of course modesty is necessary, but:

Having the mind renewed, one is safe from the lust from within.

He does not need external means to bridle his lust which would be mere external bridle! Having his mind renewed he will not say 'that woman stumbles me,' but will say that what stumbled him before the renewal of his mind was the inner lusts of his heart due to a diseased mind or to evil thoughts.

Whoever has his mind renewed will look to the body highly as serving the spirit in doing righteousness. With it, one serves and labors and even offers the body a living sacrifice acceptable to God (Rom. 12:1). The martyrs and confessors offered their bodies to God holy sacrifices, not detained by pain.

With their renewed minds they did not fear death but considered it their way to the Lord Christ.

This new mind gave the martyrs courage to face the heathen rulers and courage to edure pains and suffering considering pain as crowns over their heads. With this new mind they went to the place where they were to be martyred singing and praising God.
With the same concept when the Romans wanted to save St. Agnatius of Antioch from being cast to the hungry lions he rebuked them, saying, 'I fear your love to me would cause me harm after I had reached the end of the way.'

The same applies to fasting; a spiritual person having his mind renewed does not need to exert any effort to overcome the lust of food. Why for?

He now has an ascetic body not merely a fasting body.

His look to food and eating has changed. He now feels in fasting his spirit free, released from any restraint of the body. He has risen above material and it no more tempts him. He is progressing to attain spirituality of the body.

We put on the spiritual body in the resurrection (1 Cor. 15:44) but one gets nearer to such spirituality as far as one's nature permits.

There is a relation also between renewal of the mind and ambitions and hopes.

According to one's goals, the means will be.

If one's look to grandeur, dignity and sublimity and to success and ambition is worldly, one's behavior will be worldly as well.

A spiritual person -with renewed mind- looks to ambition in a spiritual way by which he returns to the divine image in which he was created in the beginning. Thus he sees his true status, that he is without sin as the apostle said, *"Whoever has been born of God does not sin... and he cannot sin, because he has been born of God"* (1 Jn. 3:9), *"... the wicked one does not touch him"* (1 Jn 5: 18).

With his renewed mind he says, 'How can I descend to the level of sin? How can I do this great wickedness and sin against God?' (Gen. 39:9)

With regard to success and distinction, the renewed mind has a different look.

A person with a renewed mind does not mix between success and the self, but connects between success and God's commandment. Success for him is not just a means bringing self-satisfaction and making his image lighted in the eyes of people, but he should succeed because God's children should always be successful so that God might be pleased with them. They are also successful because God is with them giving them success.

Distinction to such a person is distinction in quality not mere predominance over others.

Even if he succeeded and came first but did not attain the highest level, he will not be satisfied. He feels deficiency within. It is not for him a competition with others in which he comes first, but it is a struggle to attain perfection with all his power.

With regard to greatness, his aim is not to become great in the eyes of people, but great in the sight of the Lord as John Baptist was (Lk. 1:15).

King Herod was great in the sight of the people, but greatness involving pride. He did not give glory to God, so God permitted that an angel strike him and he was eaten by worms and died (Acts 12:21-23).

As regards John the Baptist, his greatness was due to his being filled with the Holy Spirit from his mother's womb and he used to say to people about the Lord Christ, *"He must increase, but I must decrease"* (Lk 3:30), *"... whose sandal strap I am not worthy to stoop down and loose"* (Lk. 3:16).

What is the kind of greatness which such people think of?

Is is worldly honor represented in seeking to be praised by people? Or it is the honor of humbleness as the Lord said, *"he who humbles himself will be exalted."* See what St. Antony the Great says,

[He who seeks honor, honor will fly from him, but who escapes from it wisely, it will seek him and lead people to him.]

When one's mind is renewed, one will concentrate on eternity rather than on the present world. For the apostle says, *"We do not look at the things which are seen. For the things which are seen are temporary, but the things which are not seen are eternal."* (2 Cor. 4:18)

Such a person does not do like the foolish rich man who concentrated on the good things of the present world and thought of pulling down his barns and building greater and would say to himself, *"Soul, you have many goods laid up for many years"* (Lk. 12:19). But God said to him, *"You fool! This night your soul will be required of you; then whose will those things be which you have provided?"*

He who concentrates on worldly goods is upset by tribulations.
But if his mind is renewed he will rejoice in tribulations.

With his new look he can discuss numerous blessings in tribulations as the apostle said, *"My brethren, count it all joy when you fall into various trials"* (Jas. 1:2).

Thus one takes from the tribulation the virtues of patience and forbearance and the blessing and crowns of suffering. St. Paul the anchorite said, [Who flies from tribulation flies from God.] Therefore, God commanded us to enter by the narrow gate because it leads to life (Mt. 7:13,14).

A person having a renewed mind renews his means; for there might be evil which he had thought good.

He might, while doing good, or what he thinks to be good, use wrong means such as violence, cruelty, judging or defaming others. He might be looking at the speck in the eyes of the others and not considering the plank in his own eyes.

But when his mind is renewed he will deal with matters with gentleness, mercifulness, humbleness and love, as the apostle said, *"Brethren, if a man is overtaken in any trespass, you who are spiritual restore such a one in a spirit of gentleness, considering yourself lest you also be tempted. Bear one another's burdens..."* (Gal. 6:1,2).

CHAPTER V

CONSCIENCE

MAN'S CONSCIENCE AND INFLUENCES

The conscience might err:

Conscience is not God's voice in man, and it might err or deviate, while God's voice never errs.

The conscience within man is the same like the mind or the spirit. The mind might err, and likewise the spirit and the conscience. The conscience -like any system of the body- may weaken or get stronger, it may be enlightened by the Holy Spirit, by the fathers' sayings, by preaching, by learning and by spiritual life and may weaken and slacken. It may be prevailed by some interest or by the will.

The conscience can easily go astray and its judgment changes and turns upside down. For example, a teacher may be led by his conscience to dictate the answers of the exam to a pupil, and a physician may abort a woman out of compassion or make an operation for a girl who lost her virginity or even sign a sick certificate for someone who is not sick. Likewise, a mother may cover the fault of her children by lies to save them from punishment by their father.

Amazing indeed that all these have peaceful minds and their conscience does not rebuke them! They even feel happy, thinking they have done something good.

Not being rebuked by the conscience shows a defective conscience, but feeling happy for a wrongdoing demonstrates great imbalance.

Conscience is shaped according to one's principles and ideals and changes accordingly, therefore, its judgment is not always sound. Conscience differs from one person to another; what one judges as right, another may judge as wrong and evil and vice versa.

Many examples show that conscience may be faulty and may deviate.

The Lord Christ said to His disciples, *"The time is coming that whoever kills you will think that he offers God service"* (Jn. 16: 2).

Certainly, a conscience that thinks killing the apostles a service to God is a twisted conscience.

Another example is the Roman emperors who used to give incense to their gods before going to fight their enemies and killed whoever refused to do so. Their conscience was peaceful in doing that. St. Moritius, the leader of the battalion of Thebes, was killed with all his men for the same reason: refusing to give incense to idols!

People in Pre-Islamic times fell in a similar fault; burying newly born girls alive. There are also people who offer cigarettes to their guests in funerals and feel uneasy if they do not do!! Others use microphones in a way that annoys people, does harm to the sick, interrupt students while studying, and annoy who are asleep in need of rest. Not to mention also ancient Egyptians who used to throw a beautiful girl in the Nile to please it so that it may flow with water on the Day of the Nile Inundation.

Conscience is a judge who likes good, but is not infallible.

In fact, the concept of good differs from one to the other. Besides, conscience is often influenced by many things; first of which is the kind of knowledge one aquires; lusts, affection and excitement; the impression of the community and leaders; and the power or weakness of the will.

Conscience existed before law.

Through conscience, Cain was condemned and became subject to punishment (Gen. 4) though there was not yet a commandment prohibiting killing. Through conscience also, Joseph the righteous abstained from committing adultery and said, *"How then can I do this great wickedness, and sin against God"* (Gen. 39: 9).

By conscience, there arose in the pagan world philosophers who called for good and virtue although they had no divine law, as the apostle said, *"these (Gentiles), although not having the law, are a law to themselves"* (Rom. 2: 14).

Conscience differs from one to another due to the difference of people's knowledge and difference of their mentalities and nature.

There is good conscience like a pharmacist scale; any increase or decrease therein causes harm. There is also the conscience of the Pharisees which gives concern to the letter not to the spirit. Another type of conscience is the distorted conscience or the indifferent conscience. Some people may have two consciences; by one they judge others very hard and cruelly, and by the other they judge themselves very gently and amicably!

Some conscience is affected by beliefs and traditions.

A person who worships idols is rebuked by his conscience if he does not give incense to the idol and worship it. Likewise, in some countries, a father feels an uneasy conscience if he does not kill his daughter who lost her virginity to clean out the family's honor from disgrace. The same happens when a son does not take revenge for the murder of his father by killing those who killed him.

There is a wide conscience that swallows a camel, and a narrow conscience that strains out a gnat.

A wide conscience can find a justification for many faults, whereas a narrow conscience has scruples and apprehends evil where there is none, magnifies faults and feels guilty. A person with such a conscience may think himself responsible for matters not his responsibility at all, and he sometimes feels depressed and desperate, thinking all his striving is in vain and that he will perish imagining that he has blasphemed against the Holy Spirit.

Conscience is influenced by desires

Desires and sentiments, whether love or hatred, affect the judgment and behavior of conscience. Scarcely can there be a person who judges a matter soundly without being affected by desires and sentiments.

Some people think the problems they may face can only be solved by lying.

Such a person calls lying intelligence or craft. If he judges his own behavior, he judges it very kindly, finding hundreds of justifications for that and does not judge himself severely as he does with the others. Some may call the lies white lies or joking.

Out of love for someone, a person may defend his actions however wrong they might be.

He does not feel uneasy. On the contrary, he feels uneasy if he does not defend! He considers such wrong defence a kind of faithfulness or an obligation. He might call the others to do the same and speaks very enthusiastically and fervently so that conscience can do nothing. Such a person forgets the words of the scriptures, *"He who justifies the wicked, and he who condemns the just, both of them alike are abomination to the Lord"* (Prov. 17: 15). He who justifies the wicked is against righteousness and justice. He cannot find execuse by saying that he does so out of kindness or mercy. He can rather admit the guilt then asks for compassion or mercy for the guilty. But to justify the guilty is distortion of conscience.

Sentiments may interfere in the judgments given by conscience.

Out of love for someone, a person may lie and exaggerate in praising him, feeling easy, and may lie to save him from a certain difficulty. His unhealthy conscience may even encourage him thinking that he is rendering a service to some friend.

How easy then for many to fall in the wrong principle "The end justifies the means," and their conscience accepts many wrong means under the pretext that the purpose is a noble one.

Conscience may be defective with regard to its judgments and sentiments, and in this case it does not rebuke when necessary, or blames so gently for serious matters. As someone said, 'Conscience is a just judge but is weak, and its weakness hinders enforcement of its judgments'. More dangerous still is the case where the conscience is weak and at the same time unjust.

Therefore, do not depend on your conscience alone, but consult other sound impartial consciences that are not affected by purposes, environment or leadership.

Spiritual guidance is a sound loving conscience which corrects the attitude of the conscience of the confessing person, as the scriptures say, *"There is a way which seems right to a man, but its end is the way of death"* (Prov. 14: 12).

Knowledge affects conscience:

Sound knowledge enlightens conscience and gives it understanding because many behave wrong unknowingly, and when they know they stop doing wrong.

Saul of Tarsus was a godly man who behaved wrong out of ignorance.

He said, " ... *He counted me faithful, putting me into the ministry, although I was formerly a blasphemer a persecutor, and an insolent man; but I obtained mercy because I did it ignorantly in unbelief*' (1 Tim. 1: 13). However, ignorance does not mean that a sin is not sin.

In the Trisagion we pray God to forgive our sins, which we did knowingly or unknowingly. And in the Old Testament, whenever anyone did a sin unintentionally (unknowingly), and is informed that he had sinned, he offered a sacrifice and it was forgiven him (Lev. 4).

How deep are the words of the Lord, *"My people are destroyed for lack of knowledge"* (Hos. 4: 6).

Therefore God sent prophets, apostles, masters, priests and guides to tell people about His way because the conscience became no more sufficient to guide them or it led them the wrong way.

The Holy Bible also enlightens the conscience. That is why David the Prophet said, *"Unless Your law had been my delight, I would then have perished in my affliction"* (Ps. 119: 92).

Because one's conscience may be insufficient to provide one with spiritual guidance, God provided us with father confessors and spiritual guides; for *"There is a way which seems right to a man, but its end is the way of death"* (Prov. 14: 12).

Furthermore, Satan may interfere to lead man astray as he did with our mother Eve in the past.

It is a fact then that knowledge affects conscience, whether it is good knowledge or evil knowledge.

Evil knowledge may lead the conscience as well. Did not the Epicurean philosophy based on pleasure lead the conscience of its followers?

Likewise, atheist philosophies affected the conscience of its followers, led them astray from faith and affected their conduct.

Those who confess their sins have their conscience affected by the sound faith they accepted, and those who refuse to confess -in some denominations- are also affected by the knowledge they received against confession.

Some masters teach their disciples to be completely serious and not to laugh at all, because "... *by a sad countenance the heart is made better*" (Eccl. 7: 3). Other masters teach their disciples to be cheerful and joyful, because there is "*a time to weep, and a time to laugh*" (Eccl. 3: 4). According to the kind of knowledge, conscience is affected.

For example some say that family planning is wrong, so the conscience of some people gets uncomfortable. And when some say that family planning is permissible such people feel peace of mind.

For all this, there should be one teaching in the church so that people's conscience might not be perplexed by the many contradicting doctrines they hear.

That is why church doctrines are based on receiving from the predecessors, so that teaching is kept pure and uniform. St. Paul the Apostle said, *"For I received from the Lord that which I also delivered to you"* (1 Cor. 11: 23), and said to his disciple Timothy, *"And the things that you have heard from me among many witnesses, commit these to faithful men ..."* (2 Tim. 2: 2).

Because knowledge leads conscience, a bishop is required to be able to teach (1 Tim 3: 2). And the Lord Christ rebuked the scribes and Pharisees because their teaching led people astray.

The Holy Bible tells also about false prophets and masters (Mt. 7: 15). God said to His people, *"Those who lead you cause you to err, and destroy the way of your paths"*(Isa. 3: 12; 9: 16).

People's conscience is affected by knowing good and evil and by accepting dogmatic doctrines.

The source of knowledge might be books, pamphlets or meetings. So, it is recommended to be careful when choosing the books to be read or the meetings to be attended and any readings in general.

Conscience is affected by the congregation:

Amidst people one is affected by their reactions and conscience. A person may thus act in a certain way then regrets when he returns to himself.

If a young man takes part rashly in a demonstration shouting and destroying and he is arrested and put in jail, he begins to think differently in the calmness of the prison than when he was amidst the people. Likewise, when a youth is flirting and amusing himself with some friends, his conscience only awakens and rebukes him when he gets alone.

Amidst the congregation, the people cried out, *"Away with Him! Crucify Him!"* **(Jn. 19: 15-16).**

They behaved against their conscience, led without knowing and unaware of the seriousness of what they were doing. Therefore the Lord said, while on the cross, *"Father, forgive them, for they do not know what they do"* (Lk. 23: 34). Their conscience was turned inactive by the vortex of people.

Amidst people, conscience might be led by rumours and excitement and might believe what they say and act accordingly.

Mary Magdalene is a prominent example of the influence of the congregation on one's conscience

She saw the Lord Christ, held Him by the feet and worshipped Him (Mt. 28: 9). She heard Him say, *"Go and tell My brethren to go to Galilee, and there they will see Me"* (Mt. 28: 10). However, when she came into the congregation and heard the rumours spread by the priests about stealing the holy body, she came to Simon Peter and John, saying, *"They have taken away the Lord out of the tomb, and we do not know where they have laid Him"* (Jn. 20: 2). She said the same to the two angels (Jn. 20: 13).

The conscience may be encouraged when affected by good people that lead it to good, whereas it may slacken and be inactive if surrounded by sinful people, or may change his principles and judge matters differently. This is clear in those who leave their country for a long time.

That is why the conscience of anchorites and secluded hermits are very different from those of the laity with regard to their sensitiveness, judgments and enlightment. Their consciences might even be different from those of monks living with the other monks.

However, there are some powerful consciences, like those of prophets and reformers, which are not dominated by the current of the community but rather influence it.

Such people are not affected by the corruption prevailing at their times but they lead the people and cause better changes.

But not every one is stronger than the congregation. Those powerful examples are characterized by strength, steadfastness and unsubmissiveness. They remind us of the six cataracts that obstructed the Nile and were not affected by all its currents, waves and waters along thousands of years.

Conscience is affected by leaders:

Conscience may be affected by leaders, guides, masters, famous characters and fathers.

We often find some people a typical image of their natural or spiritual fathers in the manner of behavior, in thoughts, in character, and even in movements. Such a person adopts all his father's principles, and his conscience is affected by them, they become part of his nature. This is observed in particular with the beginners and those who start forming ideals for themselves.

Conscience and will:

Conscience may conflict on its way with many things, first of which is the will.

If the will deviates towards sin and wants to do it but conscience tries to prevent this, it will try to silence the conscience or flee from its voice. Thus a struggle rises between the conscience and the will; either conscience overcomes or will overcomes, and commits sin.

Conscience is a mere voice leading the will to good and moving it away from evil, but it cannot force the will.

Suffice it to be a voice crying out continually within one's mind and heart that such or such thing is wrong. It testifies to the truth.

St. John the Baptist did not force Herod to do good, but he was just a voice crying out in Herod's face that it was not lawful for him take his brother's wife for himself. Herod did not obey the Baptist, but that great prophet remained as if he was the conscience of the whole people crying out in the face of the corrupt king, *"It is not lawful"*.

The will may try to silence the conscience under the pretext of keeping its peace!

The will does not want to let the conscience be a cause to disturb it, to make it lose its peace and comfort. So it silences the conscience.

Such an ill will is also concerned about its own comfort not the comfort of the spirit, because the spirit finds its comfort in obeying the Lord and in the purity of the heart, and it accepts rebuking, unlike the will which cannot accept rebuking.

The will may flee from the conscience and not give it a chance to work.

It flees from self-examination and from rebuking of conscience through continual involvement. When the voice of conscience comes from outside, from the father or from a friend or master, it tries to change the talk to another subject. The voice of conscience makes the self uncomfortable, so it flees from it.

Conscience may find no place for itself and it keeps silent and submits. Time passes and conscience gets used to silence and does not interfere with the acts of the will.

The will remains alone in the field, doing whatever it wants and realizes its wishes giving no chance to the conscience to work. Conscience thus becomes non existent, hidden or asleep and does not carry out its function of giving guidance.

The various means of entertainment and amusement, the dominance of sin, the continual involvement, the useless rebuking, the despair of conscience or the continual promise to repent afterwards, all this encourages conscience to keep silent.

In this way it seems useless and the will wins over the conscience and remains in sin because the conscience is a mere guide that does not force the will to accept its advice.

The conscience is like traffic signals which gives red light to drivers to stop but do not force them to do.

How easy it is for a driver to disobey the red traffic signal and continue driving even though he is charged for contravention, but his is indifferent. The conscience is a mere guide, whereas enforcement is in the hand of the will.

But what happens if the will deviates and silences the conscience? Would man perish? Here God's will interferes and sends His grace to save man from his own will.

Since man's conscience is weak, and the deviating will prevails, there should be an external power that interferes and saves him. Here appears God's Holy Spirit, and the fruit of the prayers of angels and saints. The grace works to awaken the inattentive person and softens his hard heartedness.

Saint Mary the Coptic, for example, while deeply in sin, not thinking at all of repentance but longing to other sins by which she can trap many, the grace attracted her in Jerusalem. She soon responded to the work of grace and repented. She even became a great saint and deserved to give blessing to Zosima the priest!

Grace may interfere by itself as a result of a visitation from the Holy Spirit or in response to a prayer requesting God's help.

Perhaps the sinner himself prays and cries out to God saying, *"restore me, and I will return"* (Jer. 31: 18). The prayer may come from those who love him and who ask for his salvation, or from the spirits of the holy people who departed.

It needs our prayers that the divine help might interfere.

People cannot be saved by mere sermons. Sermons may move the conscience, but still the will may not move towards good!

We need hearts that pour in prayer before God that He may work within the sinner and attract him to His way; for as the apostle says, *"for to will is present with me, but how to perform what is good I do not find. For the good that I will to do, I do not do; but the evil I will not to do, that I practice"* (Rom. 7: 18, 19).

There is a beautiful story in the Book of Zechariah the Prophet about Joshua who was standing before the angel of the Lord with filthy garments while Satan was standing at his right hand to oppose him. Then the Lord said to Satan, *"The Lord rebuke you, Satan! Is this not a brand plucked from the fire?"* (Zech. 3: 2), and God saved Joshua.

Though grace interferes, man remains free to respond or refuse the work of grace. He can open to the Lord who stands knocking at his door (Rev. 3: 20) or refuse to open. He may accept the work of the Spirit or grieves Him, quenches His fervence or resists Him!

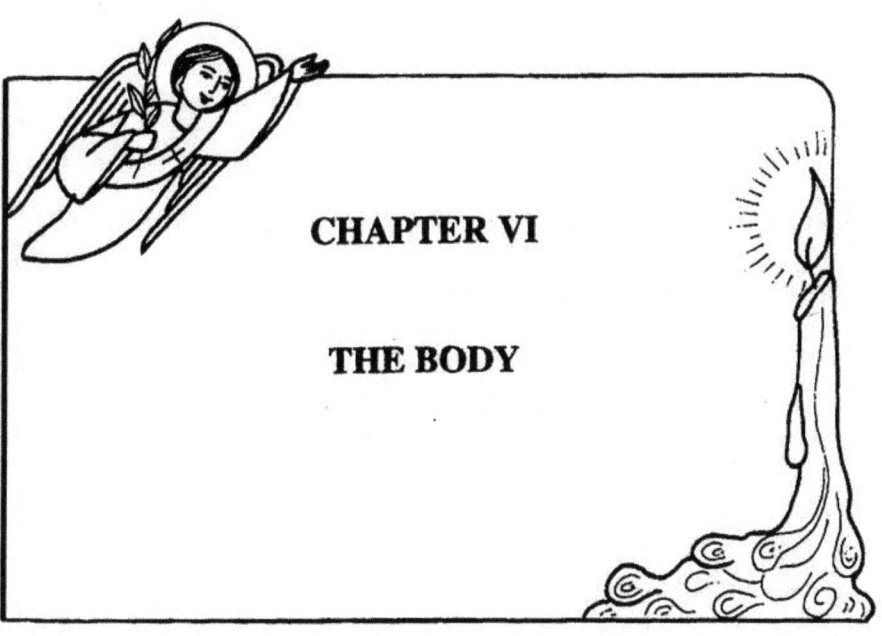

CHAPTER VI

THE BODY

A CHRISTIAN PERSPECTIVE OF THE BODY

During fast we train ourselves to subject our bodies, but is the body evil or good?

The body is not evil:

The body is not in itself evil for many reasons:

1. Had the body been evil, God would not have created it. We notice also that when God created man with a body, *"God saw everything that He had made, and indeed it was very good"* (Gen. 1: 31).

2. Had the body been evil, the Lord Christ would not have incarnated and taken a body like ours *"And the Word became flesh"* (Jn. 1: 14).

3. Had the body been evil, it would not have been written, *"Or do you not know that your body is the temple of the Holy Spirit who is in you"* (1 Cor. 6: 19), and, *"Do you not know that your bodies are members of Christ?"* (1 Cor. 6: 15).

4. Were the body evil, God would not raise it!! It would be sufficient for man to bear it in this world and not carry it in eternity too!!

5. Were the body evil, God would not glorify it in His resurrection raising it a spiritual heavenly body (1 Cor. 15: 44, 49). He raised it in power and in glory, putting on incorruption (1 Cor. 15: 43, 53). He even glorified it after His glorious body as the apostle says, *"who will transform our lowly body that it may be conformed to His glorious body"* (Phil. 3: 21).

6. Were the body evil, we would not honor the bodies and relics of the saints and consider them holy and blessed, and wonders are worked in the church by them.

7. Were the body evil, the Holy Bible would not say, *"I beseech you therefore, ... that you present your bodies a living sacrifice, holy, acceptable to God"* (Rom. 12: 1), and, *"glorify God in your body and in your spirit, which are God's"* (1 Cor. 6: 20).

However, there is much said in the Holy Bible against the body (Rom. 8), against the works of the flesh (Gal. 5: 19) and against setting the mind on the things of the flesh and walking according to the flesh (Rom. 8: 1-9).

Which body is meant here? It is not the body itself, in general, but the sinful body.

The sinful body:

A sinful body is that which resists the spirit.

The apostle says, *"For the flesh lusts against the spirit, and the spirit against the flesh; and these are contrary to one another, so that you do not do the things that you wish"* (Gal. 5: 17).

Many examples of the works of this sinful body are mentioned by the apostle in (Gal. 5: 19-21).

A sinful body is the lustful body.

The lusts of the body are material or filthy. Therefore, the apostle says, *"Walk in the Spirit, and you shall not fulfill the lust of the flesh"* (Gal. 5: 16). The lust of the body might be, *"adultery, fornication, uncleanness, licentiousness"* (Gal. 5: 19), and might be gluttony as for food and drink. Lust might also be for sensual matters which turn into habit or addiction like smoking and drugs.

A sinful body is that which is so concerned with material that it is subjected to it.

The apostle said in this regard, *"The carnal mind is enmity against God"*, *"For to be carnally minded is death, but to be spiritually minded is life and peace"* (Rom. 8: 7, 6).

The Lord Himself said about this, *"do not worry about your life, what you will eat or what you will drink; nor about your body, what you will put on"* (Mt. 6: 25), and also, *"Do not lay up for yourselves treasures on earth ... but lay up for yourselves treasures in heaven"* (Mt. 6: 19).

The sinful body leads the spirit and the soul to sin.

When the senses sin, the spirit and the soul take part and the whole person is defiled; body and soul, as the Lord says, *"whoever looks at a woman to lust for her has already committed adultery with her in his heart"* (Mt. 5: 28). All work together, the body through the eyes, the soul through lusting and the spirit represented by the heart.

Look how Solomon did sin when he obeyed the lust of the body!

Solomon said, *"I built myself houses, and planted myself vineyards. I made myself gardens and orchards ... I also gathered for myself silver and gold ... I acquired male and female singers, the delights of the sons of men ... whatever my eyes desired I did not keep from them"* (Eccl. 2: 4-10).

Thus Solomon led a carnal life and fell because of the women (1 Kgs. 11), and as it written, *"his wives turned his heart after other gods; and his heart was not loyal to the Lord his God"* (1 Kgs. 11: 4).

Solomon's body could cast his spirit into the depth of sin.
He did not glorify God neither with his spirit nor with his body but fell as a whole!

How deep indeed are the words said by Saint Paul the Apostle,
"O wretched man that I am! Who will deliver me from this body of death?" (Rom. 7: 24).

Sinful members:

One member only of the body many sins, but it defiles the whole body and the spirit altogether.

Take the tongue, for example, which is only a small member

As St. James the apostle says, *"Even so the tongue is a little member and boasts great things. See how great a forest a little fire kindles! And the tongue is a fire, a world of iniquity ... it defiles the whole body, and sets on fire the course of nature; and it is set on fire by hell"* (Jas. 3: 5, 6).

See then how many are the sins in which one falls as a result of the tongue slips, as the Holy Bible says, *"For by your words you will be justified, and by your words you will be condemned"* (Mt. 12: 37).

By the tongue a person is defiled as the Lord says, *"What comes out of the mouth, this defiles a man"* (Mt. 15: 11).

As we mention the tongue which defiles, we should also mention the eye.

As St. James the apostle said that friendship with the world is enmity with God (Jas. 4: 4), so also St. John the apostle said, *"If anyone loves the world, the love of the Father is not in him. For all that is in the world- the lust of the flesh, the lust of the eyes, and the pride of life ..."* (1 Jn. 2: 15, 16).

The lust of the eyes trapped our mother Eve; for when she saw the tree she found it was pleasant to the eyes and desirable (Gen. 3: 6).

Many are the sins in which the eye falls.

When one looks with lust, with anger or malice, with envy or revenge, with pride or deadain, with deceit or cruelty, or with any other sinful look, the image of that sinful looks appears clear in the eyes.

Many other members do sin as well.

The hand may beat, kill or steal, or do similar sins.

The foot may walk to the places of sin . The features of the face may reveal inner pride, anger or cruelty.

For all this we shall speak about subjecting the body.

Subjecting the body:

The most important and significant verse on subjecting the body is probably that said by St. Paul the Apostle, *"But I discipline my body and bring it into subjection, lest, when I have preached to others, I myself should become disqualified"* (1 Cor. 9: 27). How fearful are these words especially when said by the saint who was caught up to the third heaven (2 Cor. 12:2), and who labored more abundantly than all the apostles (1 Cor. 15: 10). This shows us how dangerous the body is, and how important it is to subject and discipline it.

Another significant verse in this regard is that said by the same apostle also, *"And those who are Christ's have crucified the flesh with its passions and desires"* (Gal. 5: 24).

These words mean that we should nail and crucify every desire of the body contradicting the spirit, so that such desire might not move again.

The virtue of fasting is one of the important means of subjecting the body.

It is a virtue which subjects the body whether through abstaining from food and enduring hunger, or through abstaining from taking the foods one desires, as Daniel the Prophet said about his fast, *"I ate no pleasant food, no meat or wine came into my mouth"* (Da. 10: 3). If you cannot abstain completely, at least take the least you can.

As you prevent your body from food, prevent it also from other desires.

Controlling senses and tongue are other means of subjecting the body.

Control your looks, your smelling and touching senses as the Lord said in the Sermon on the Mount, *"And if your right eye causes you to sin, pluck it out and cast it from you ... And if your right hand causes you to sin, cut if off and cast it from you"* (Mt. 5: 29, 30).

Watching is another means of controlling the body.

The watching we mean is that for prayer and worship as the Lord said, *"Watch and pray, lest you enter into temptation"* (Mt. 26: 41), and as one of the holy fathers said, 'Force yourself to keep the night prayer, and pray more psalms'.

Among the means of controlling the body is asceticism & piety

We mean by asceticism & piety at least avoiding amusement and luxury, and avoiding excessive worldly adornment. The apostle concentrated on the ornament of a gentle and quiet spirit, *"which is very precious in the sight of God"* (1 Pet. 3: 4). The spirit should adorn itself with virtues to be as the Song says, *"perfumed with myrrh and frank incense, with all the merchant's fragrant powders"* (Song 3: 6).

Man should know that the body is not for enjoyment and entertainment

The body is for glorifying God, as the apostle said, *"glorify God in your body and in your spirit, which are God's"* (1 Cor. 6: 20).

How should we glorify God with our bodies?

1. The body can work with the spirit:

When the spirit prays, the body takes part by standing solemnly, raising the hands, keeping the senses, kneeling and prostrating. Some may wrongly think that God is concerned with the hearts only, so they do not care for making the body take part!! They may even pray while sitting or lying in the bed!! Some people from other countries do not put off their shoes when going into the sanctuary. They forget that the Holy Bible said, *"Take your sandals off your feet, for the place where you stand is holy ground"* (Ex. 3: 5), (Jash. 5: 15).

2. We glorify God when we labor in His service:

The apostle said about his ministry, *"in labors, in sleeplessness, in fastings"* (2 Cor. 6: 15), and, *"in labors more abundant ... in journeys often ... in perils in the wilderness, in perils in the sea ... in weariness and toil, in sleeplessness often, in hunger and thirst, in fastings often, in cold and nakedness ..."* (2 Cor. 11: 23-27).

Our holy fathers, in giving themselves in the service, were candles melting to give light to others. That is why we light candles in front of the icons of the saints. Their life was a light, they gave themselves in the service and worship of God.

3. The father martyrs no doubt glorified God with their bodies:

The church put the martyrs in a rank above other saints because they suffered much for His sake, and it is written, *"if indeed we suffer with Him, that we may also be glorified together"* (Rom. 8: 17).

4. We can glorify Him at least by the labor of the body:

St. Paul wearied much in the body by asceticism and spiritual struggle until the Lord appeared to him and said, "Suffice you this labor, My beloved Paul". But the saint replied Him, 'what is the value of this labor if compared to what You have done and given for us, O Lord'.

5. We glorify God by the purity of our bodies:

God's Holy Spirit dwells within us when He finds our bodies holy temples for Him. With such purity of the body we introduce to the people the divine image and we can thereby deserve to partake of the holy sacraments which do also purify us.
Chastity and modesty are aspects of purity.

Bodies of the Saints:

The saints who glorified God in their bodies, their bodies were glorified by God.

An example of this is the body of the holy Virgin which God raised to the heaven.

God gave honor to these bodies so that even the bones of Elisha the prophet was very blessed and raised the dead who touched them (2 Kgs. 13: 21).

God glorified the bodies of the saints even while still alive

This is apparent from the following examples:

- Moses face shone after he had met the Lord God on the mount so that the people were afraid and could not come near to him and he put a veil on his face (Ex. 34: 30-35).

- St. Stephen's face when he was brought to the council - was shining *"And all who sat in the council, ... saw his face as the face of an angel"* (Acts 6: 15).

- The handkerchiefs and aprons brought from St. Paul's body cured the diseases and cast out the evil spirits (Acts 19: 12).

CHAPTER VII

THE HEART

THE HEART PLAYS A ROLE IN EVERY ACTION

The importance of the heart:

A remarkable example of the importance of the heart can be found in the Book of Proverbs, it says,

> *"Keep your heart with all diligence.*
> *For out of it spring the issues of life"* **(Prov. 4: 23)**

Everything comes out of the heart, and that expresses the reality of the person, his inner heart and intentions. God knows everything in man's heart; *"He weights the hearts"* (Prov. 21: 2), *"He tests the hearts"* (Ps. 7: 9) (Prov. 2: 23)

The heart is the center of the feelings, the center of the sentiments, and the center of love, and God loves these feelings and heart sentiments.
That is why He said,
"My son, give me your heart" (Prov. 23: 26) And the natural result is that *"your eyes observe My ways"*.

Spiritual life is not mere practices of worship, or outward virtues, but rather an inner life; a life of a heart attached in love to God. All the virtues, worship, and practices come from that heart adorned with the sign of love.

Spiritual life is not mere outer practices by man nor mere law-in other words, commandments to be obeyed literally- but it is, primarily, the life of the heart with God.

How beautiful are the words of the psalm in this respect,
"The royal daughter is all glorious within" (Ps. 45)
Although her clothing is woven with gold and her robes are in many colors, all her glory lies within; in her heart and spirit.

Now, let us see the relationship between the heart and the feeling, the tongue, the mind and the will, and with repentance, worship and the whole life with God.

The heart is the source of feelings:

In the heart we find either kindness and goodness, or hardness and severity;
Either faith and trust, or suspicion and lack of peace;

In the heart there may be humbleness and gentleness as the Lord Christ was gentle and lowly in heart (Mt. 11: 29).
But do not think that humbleness means to utter humble words such as 'I am a sinner, I do not deserve anything'; for a person may say this but cannot bear others to say to him 'You are a sinner'!!

True humbleness is a humbled heart, and pride is arrogance of the heart.
The first sin in the world was a sin of the heart, a sin of pride.

By this sin Satan fell, by haughtiness of the heart. Thus the Lord rebuked him, saying:

"For you have said in your heart: 'I will ascend into heaven. I will exalt my throne above the stars of God ... I will be like the Most High" (Isa. 14: 13, 14)

It is written concerning pride, *"Pride goes before destruction. And a haughty spirit before a fall"* (Prov. 16: 18). It is therefore a sin within man, in his heart before taking an outer form.

The heart also has fear as well as confidence.

The same event occurs to two different persons: one of them feels afraid, trembles, and imagines dreadful things, whereas the other faces it with peace and confidence, and thinks calmly how to avoid bad results. According to the heart a person feels. So the psalm says, *"Be of good courage, and He shall strengthen your heart"* (Ps. 27: 14).

The heart contains everything within you and from you.

The heart is the source of all virtues as well as the source of all sins.

The words your tongue utters are ascribed to the heart; for, *"Out of the abundance of the heart the mouth speaks"* (Mt. 12: 34). Not only the words but also the thoughts come out of the heart, *"A good man out of the good treasure of his heart brings forth good, and an evil man out of the evil treasure of his heart brings forth evil"* (Lk. 6: 45).

If your heart is filled with love, it will appear in your dealings, and if filled with enmity or hatred, this will appear in your behavior and even in your voice and your looks. The heart is the source of all this, unless there is also hypocrisy and a person shows what is not truly within him. But even this is revealed.

The heart and the mind:

The heart and the mind work together, each is a cause and a result.

The heart feelings bring forth thoughts in the mind, and the mind causes feelings in the heart. If you desire to sin, this desire will bring you sinful thoughts. And if you think of sin, the heart will bring you sinful lusts.

If you want a good heart, rectify your thoughts and avoid the sources of sinful thoughts.

Avoid thoughts that come to you from books, from senses, from bad company, or from other sources. In this way the thoughts will not press on your heart and you will attain an upright good heart.

The existentialists who rejected God in their hearts, accepted atheism in their minds. Atheism may thus be from the mind and heart together.

You might have good relationship with someone, then a third might change your mind against him and you find your heart also changed. With the change of the heart, the features and dealings change also!

If you say: I want to give my heart to God. I'll tell you: Give Him your mind also.

Wherever your heart is, your mind will be there, and the apposite is true. Therefore, it is well stated in the Holy Bible, *"You shall love the Lord you God with all your heart, with all your soul, and with all your mind"* (Mt. 22: 37).

Renewal of the mind brings forth renewal of the heart.

Thus the apostle says, *"... be transformed by the renewing of your mind"* (Rom. 12: 2). If new thoughts are introduced into your mind, and you are convinced with and believed in them, you will be changed accordingly in form and heart. Your conscience will take another path by which it will lead your heart.

This is the role of preaching in renewing the mind and the heart.

With the change of the mind and the heart, the tongue will also change. All this certainly has its effects on the will.

The heart and the will:

When God's love fills one's heart, one cannot do wrong because God's love prevails on one's behavior. Thus the will tends completely toward God.

On the contrary, if the heart is not straight in his love of God, his will will be shaken.

The will, in this case, will behave according to the outer influences whether good or evil. Therefore it is written, *"You will love the Lord your God with all your heart"*. The word *"all"* has its significance.

When all the heart is devoted to God, the whole will is certainly devoted to Him.

Likewise, if the heart is serious, strict and committed to values and principles, so also will be the person's will.

An inconstant heart has a changeable will.

There is then a connection between the heart and the mind, between the heart and the tongue, between the heart ant the will, and between the heart and virtue.

The heart and the tongue:

Whatever you utter comes from the heart as the Holy Bible says,
"For out of the abundance of the heart the mouth speaks" **(Mt. 12: 34).**
The Lord explains this, saying, "*A good man out of the good treasure of his heart brings forth good; and an evil man out of his heart brings forth evil*" (Lk. 6: 45).
This is the fact, unless what comes out is hypocrisy not from the heart, as when a person speaks what is not in his heart or opposite to it. In this case, if you say a good word by your mouth and your heart says the opposite, God will judge you

according to your heart, not according to what you said by your tongue.

You will add to the sin of the heart the sin of hypocrisy.

God, who will judge you on the Last Day, tests the mind and the heart (Jer. 11: 20).

The scribes and the Pharisees, the hypocrites, spoke good words though they were evil.

Their words availed them nothing; for the Lord condemned them and uttered woes against them (Mt. 23). The Lord said about them that they *"cleanse the outside of the cup and dish, but inside they are full of extortion and self-indulgence"*, and that they are *"like whitewashed tombs which indeed appear beautiful outwardly, but inside are full of dead men's bones and all uncleanness"* (Mt. 23: 25, 27).

What lies in the heart is the important thing as the psalm says,
"The royal daughter is all glorious within" (Ps. 45: 13). Although her clothing is woven with gold and her robes are of many colors, yet what avails is that which is within. Soft words alone are not effective unless they express true feelings of the heart. Otherwise the words of the psalm shall apply to them, *"The words of his mouth were smoother than butter ... Yet they were drawn swords"* (Ps. 55: 21).

You may apologize to someone, but he does not accept it well.

This might be because he feels that your words are not from the heart but rather mere words. You may say 'I am sorry', but your voice does not express your sorrow and regret. Your words are not combined with the feelings of your heart, thus, they are unvaluable and unacceptable.

A quick person can easily find out the reality behind the words and whether they are from the heart or not.

The voice reveals the words whether they are words of praise, of apology or of advice. The features also reveal the reality. Anything in the heart can be revealed and found out; words cannot conceal it.

How deep is the importance of the heart for the relationship with God and with people!

Life with God:

Your life with God begins within the heart.

It begins with faith; which is an act of the heart.

Through faith you trust in God's presence in general, and in His presence in your life in particular. In life with Him you will rely on Him as the Wise Solomon said, *"Trust in the Lord with all your heart, and lean not on your understanding"* (Prov. 3: 5). With this trust you give Him your life, confident that He will lead it well. All this is feelings of the heart. In your life with Him you say to Him always,
"My heart is steadfast,
O God, my heart is steadfast" (Ps. 57: 7).

We repeat this sentence in the second psalm of the sixth hour prayer psalms. We want to say that we are steadfast and ready to accept God's work with us, ready to accept communion with the Holy Spirit who dwells in our hearts, and ready to obey His commandments as the Lord Himself requires us, *"Let your heart keep My commands"* (Prov. 3: 1).

The Psalmist also says,
"Your word I have hidden in my heart, that I might not sin against You" (Ps. 119: 11).

It means that God's commands should be in the heart, in the action of the feelings, in the emotions, thus we shall not sin.

When God gave the people His commandments, He said, *"And these words which I command you today shall be in your heart; you shall teach them diligently to your children, and shall talk of them when you sit in your house"* (Deut. 6: 6). Thus, if God's words are in the heart, one can meditate in them day and night, as God commanded Joshua (Josh. 1: 8), and as said in the First Psalm about the righteous,
"His delight is in the law of the Lord, and in His law he meditates day and night" (Ps. 1: 2).

If God's words (law) have become one's delight, it means that they have become loved by him, that is, have entered into his heart. David the Prophet talked much about such love, and repeated it in his prayers, singing for God's precepts and statutes, *"they are the rejoicing of my heart"*; *"How sweet are Your words to my taste, sweeter than honey to my mouth!"*, *"I *have rejoiced in the way of Your testimonies, as much as in all riches "* ...

God's commandment becomes difficult for us, if we keep it away from our hearts, if we do not mix it with our emotions so that we might feel its beauty and love it.

Your heart is the cause:

If you say, 'I am lost because of <u>so and so</u>, I say to you, 'It is your heart that caused this'

If you were strong, not easily shaken, he would not be able to do that. Such a person can only fight you from without ; and if within is sound, you will not be injured. A house built on the rock will not fall by rain, by floods, or by winds; for it is founded on the rock (Mt. 7: 25). The ark was surrounded by heavy waters but the waters could not drown it, because there was no hole through which water could come into, and because God was in it.

True indeed are the words of St. John Chrysostom,
[No one can hurt a person unless such a person hurts himself].

You might say: The words I heard changed my thoughts and made be suspect!

But I tell you that your heart was ready to accept suspicions. If your heart were steadfast, suspicions would not enter into it, no matter what words you heard.

Around the crucified Lord there were two thieves; one of them blasphemed, and the other believed in Him as Lord and King, confessed this and entered into Paradise (Lk. 23: 39-43). Both were thieves, and both were in the same circumstances, but the heart of one was different from that of the other.

Did Thomas doubt in his heart, or only by his words?

Certainly, the doubt was in his heart, not in his tongue nor in his finger which he wanted to put in the wounds!

You might say: Tribulations shook me!
But I say to you: Had your heart been strong, it would not have been shaken by tribulations.

I told you before that a tribulation troubles a narrow heart, but an open heart is not troubled by anything, as St. Paul said to the Corinthians, *"O Corinthians! We have spoken openly to you, our heart is wide open. You are not restricted by us, but you are restricted by your own affections. Now in return for the same, I speak as to children, you also be open"* (2 Cor. 6: 11-13).

An open heart handles any problem and solves it by taking the blessing of facing it, then referring it to God who solves it.

Spiritual features of the heart:
* First there is **the pure heart** which the Lord has blessed in the beatitudes, *"Blessed are the pure in heart"* (Mt. 5: 8). The apostle also mentioned it, *"Now the purpose of the commandment is love from a pure heart, from a good conscience ..."* (1 Tim. 1: 5).

* There is also **the true heart** (Heb. 10: 22).

* The apostle mentions also **The sincerity of heart** (Col. 3: 22).

* The psalmist tells us about **the steadfast heart** that trusts in the Lord (Ps. 112: 7).

* There is also **the broken and contrite heart** which God will not despise, and which is better than sacrifices (Ps. 50: 17).

* The Lord Christ said of Himself that He is gentle and **lowly in heart** (Mt. 11: 29).

On the other hand, the Holy Bible warns us against the **hardness of the heart** (Mt. 19: 8) (Ezek. 3: 7), and against the **deceitful heart** (Prov. 17: 20).

As we are concerned about purity of the heart, we should also mention the relationship between the heart and repentance.

I would talk to you about such a relationship and about the positive work in the spiritual life and its relationship with prayer and worship, but time is lacking!

THE HEART & ITS SPIRITUAL WORK

The heart and repentance:

True repentance is that which comes from the heart.
Repentance that comes from the will alone is not true repentance, because the will might sometimes be strong and in other times weak. The will might be strong enough to abstain from sinning, yet the love of sin remains within the heart, thus it is not true repentance. Perfect repentance is hatred of sin; which is the work of the heart.

The Lord said, *"Return to Me, and I will return to you"* (Mal. 3: 7).

"Turn to Me with all your heart" (Joel 2: 12).

This is the true return because so long as there is a beloved sin in the heart, there will be no true repentance. The Scriptures connect between the repentance and the new heart that is renewed by repentance, as the Lord says,

"I will give you a new heart and put a new spirit within you" (Ezek. 36: 26).

The words *"new heart"* mean new in its emotions and desires, and in its attachment to God with new desires, new intentions and new concepts. This is the kind of true repentance of which the psalmist said,

"With my whole heart I have sought You" (Ps. 119: 10).

Of this kind of repentance the Lord said,

"So rend your heart, and not your garments; return to the Lord your God" (Joel 2: 13); *"Cast away from you all the transgressions which you have committed, and get yourselves a new heart and a new spirit"* (Ezek. 18: 31); and, *"Then I will give them a heart to know Me"* (Jer. 24: 7).

David the prophet also, feeling the importance of the heart for repentance, says in the psalm of repentance, *"Create in me a clean heart, O God"* (Ps. 51: 10).

Repentance is closely related to the purity of the heart. It implies return of the heart to God, and when the heart returns to God, the will becomes strong and able to get rid of sin. The problem of remaining under domination of sin in spite of the attempt to forsake it, is due to the fact that the will tries alone to attain repentance while the heart does not wish.

It is the repentance from the heart that continues.

On the other hand, repentance which is mere promises from the mouth does not continue long since the heart has not the love of God in it nor did it hate sin yet. That is why the Holy Bible looks at non repentance as hard-heartedness, as St. Paul the Apostle says,

"Today, if you will hear His voice, do not harden your hearts" (Heb. 3: 7, 8).

These same words are repeated thrice on the same occasion as in (Heb. 3: 15) and in (Heb. 4: 7). It is because a hard heart, void of any feelings of love towards God is not at all ready to accept God's work in it nor to respond to the communion of the Spirit. It is unbending cruel heart like that of Pharaoh which none of the miracles, the wonders and the plagues did have any effect on him.

A person who does not obey the voice of God is a hard hearted person.

Repentance is not mere words uttered by the tongue, but rather a change in the heart as the Lord said in the Book of Ezekeil.

True repentance is a a change in the heart, and a change in one's inner desires.

It means that one desires good instead of sin; for true repentance is not mere outward abstention from doing sin while the heart desires it within!!
It is turning to God with all the heart as He said in (Joel 2: 12).

In the life of repentance, put before you this fact:
If you overcome within, in the heart, you will overcome without also.

You might say there are stumbling blocks, temptations and wars outside! Never mind, but let your heart be overcoming within and none of all this will affect it. Joseph the righteous was overcoming within and offences, temptations and wars had no influence on him.

Do you say that so and so aroused your anger? You would better say, 'He revealed to me the sin of my heart, because had my heart been strong, I would have not fallen in anger'.

A sin is repeated when the heart holds fast to it.

Likewise, spiritual talk about repentance is of no avail since the heart does not desire it, or refuses it because of being attached to sinful love.

Outer offences have influence and may lead to sin if the heart responds to them. But if the heart rejects offences, it will not be offended by them while others might be if they do accept them. So, any change comes from the heart.

Overcoming sin is an internal action.

If you comment on a girl's clothing, appearance or make up, or on a young man's long hair or tight pants, trying to press on them or even rebuking and blaming but leaving the heart as it is, this will certainly have no effect whatsoever. What avails is the heart within, the inner conviction of the mind and heart.

See what St. Paul the apostle says,

"be transformed by the renewing of your mind" (Rom. 12: 2)

Outer change should be a result of internal renewal, out of a mind thinking in a different way, in a spiritual way that arouses the heart and the feelings. When preaching, we should address people's hearts rather than their ears so that both mind and heart might change.

Amazingly enough, most people confess their outer faults only and do not confess what lies in the heart!

A person may get angry, aroused and may insult and judge others, then confesses these sins only, scarcely confessing that his heart has no love or forbearance, has no meekness, gentleness or humbleness, lacks respect to others and caring for their feelings.

Would we then disregard the sins of the heart and concentrate on the sins of the tongue!

The sins of the tongue are due to internal sins of the heart, because out of the abundance of the heart the mouth speaks (Lk. 6: 45). I wonder that when someone does sin, some people might say: Truly, he is wrong but his heart is white!! No, brothers, a white heart speaks white (good) words and vice versa.

Sometimes we concentrate on the sins of the senses or action, forgetting the sins of the heart!!

We usually say that the sin of our mother Eve was that she disobeyed God, took of the fruit of the tree, ate and gave her husband to eat, and we forget that it was a sin of the heart that led to all this, a heart that gave place to lust after listening to the words of the serpent. When the heart changed, the senses changed and the look of the woman changed as her heart lost its purity and simplicity, so she found that the tree was *"good for food, it was pleasant to the eyes, and a tree desirable ..."* (Gen. 3: 6). The tree was in front of them everyday and they never saw it like that!!

The look changed by the change of the heart.

When lust entered into the heart, the senses began to desire. Thus the sin of the senses is a second sin whereas the sin of the heart is the first.

See what the Lord says in the Sermon on the Mount about adultery,

"Whoever looks at a woman to lust for her has already committed adultery with her in his heart" (Mt. 5: 28).

It means that adultery exists first in the heart before moving to the senses. It is the bad lust of the heart that defiles the look. Would we then consider it a sin of the sight or of the heart? It is a sin of the heart that led to a sin of the sight. If the heart is pure there will be no lust of the senses.

The first sin that came into the world was a sin of the heart.

It was the sin of Satan whose heart was lifted up. He said in his heart, *"I will ascend into heaven. I will exalt my throne above the stars of God .... I will be like the Most High"* (Isa. 14: 13, 14). This reminds us also of the sin of Nebuchadnezzar whose heart was lifted up (Da. 5: 20).

Positive work of the heart:

After we had talked about the wrong feelings of the heart, we should talk about the heart's positive role with regard to virtue.

Take for example the enthusiasm and holy zeal in the heart

These are the source of every successful service. People might talk about aspects and results of the service, but the important thing is the internal condition of the heart; it is the cause. The inner feelings of the heart make the difference between the zealous fiery service and the routine service. What avails also is how far the heart is convinced of the importance of salvation and how committed it is to work on spreading the Kingdom.

There is also the fruits of the Spirit within the heart (Gal. 5: 22, 23).

The first fruit which the apostle mentions is love. How important is the hearty love of God and people, on which all the law and prophets hang as the Lord Christ said (Mt. 22: 40).

Love is an action of the heart and the source of every good. Therefore it is written,
***"You shall love the Lord your God with all your heart, with all your soul, and with all your mind"* (Mt. 22: 37) (Deut. 6: 5)**

If you attain such love, you will have attained the top and you are no more under the law. Every fear in the heart will be removed because *"perfect love casts out fear"* (1 Jn. 4: 18).

We cannot speak about outward obedience of the commandments and forget the love of the Lord!

Nay, Love is the basis, and every obedience of the commandment -without love- will be nothing in God's eyes as the apostle teaches us (1 Cor. 13). Such love lifts man above the level of the world, the material and the flesh and makes him attached to God solely as the spiritual father said [God's love estranged me from the humans and every human practice].

This is the depth of the monastic life.

Monasticism is not mere consecration, black garments or certain appearance. It is, first of all, death of the heart to the world or death of the world inside the heart. With this feeling, the saints gave themselves as martyrs.

Martyrdom was within the heart before the body was tortured or killed.

The heart and worship:

God looks at the heart and is interested in it, therefore, He said,
"My son, give me your heart" (Prov. 23: 26).
And when the heart is given to God, the eyes will observe His ways.

Some people give formal worship to God. They appear as if they are observing His ways while they do not give Him their hearts. An example of those are the scribes and the Pharisees who seem keen on obeying the commandment while their hearts are far away from God! About those and others similar to them the Lord said,
"This people honors Me with their lips, but their heart is far from Me" (Mk. 7: 6).

God never accepted worship from such people. He said about those who practice outer rituals but their hearts are defiled within, *"Bring no more futile sacrifices ... Your New Moons and your appointed feasts My soul hates; they are a trouble to Me. I am weary of bearing them. When you spread out your hands, I will hide My eyes from you; even though you make many prayers, I will not hear. Your hands are full of blood"* (Isa. 1: 13-15).

Sometimes you set for yourself a spiritual schedule according to which you examine yourself with regard to spiritual practices such as prayer, fasting, readings, prostrations, contemptations ... etc .;

But do you examine yourself only with regard to practices, or examine your heart?

You may put a mark indicating that you have read the Holy Bible on a certain day while your heart did not really take part in the reading. The same with praying while your heart did not take part, or with fasting which was not by all your heart and your heart did not abstain from lusts. Would it be then a schedule for your spiritual life truly whereas your heart has no role in it?

An acceptable prayer is that from the heart.

An acceptable prayer is not mere words uttered before God. That is why we sing in the Praise Hymn "My heart and tongue give praise to the Holy One", that is, not the tongue alone.

Likewise, when you go to church, do you go by your feet alone or by your heart as well? See what the psalmist says:

"I was glad when they said to me, 'Let us go into the house of the Lord' " (Ps. 122: 1).

Gladness is of course a heart feeling.

And also the reading of the Holy Bible, when it is from the heart, you will say with the psalmist, *"I rejoice at Your word as one who finds great treasure"* (Ps. 119: 162). Thus you will not keep God's words only in your mind but will let them enter your heart as David said in the psalm,

*"Your word I have hidden in my heart,
that I might not sin against You"* (Ps. 119: 11).

The Lord God commands us to do the same when giving His commandments, He said, *"And these words which I command you today shall be in your heart; you shall teach them diligently to your children, and shall talk of them when you sit in your house"* (Deut. 6: 6, 7). First you should keep them in your heart, not only in your ears or even in your mind.

The heart and prayer:

Prayer is not mere words we utter before God, nor mere talk with God. It is rather feelings of a heart poured before God even without words. That is why the psalmist said,

*"I will lift up my hands in Your name.
My soul will be satisfied as with marrow and fatness"* (Ps. 63: 4, 5).

If mere lifting of the hands, without words is so effective, how much more the words would be!

In the prayer of the Pharisee and the tax collector; The Pharisee talked much but his heart was not with God, so his prayer was not accepted. But the tax collector said one sentence only with contrite heart and he *"went down to his house justified rather than the other"* (Lk. 18: 14).

In the same way the single sentence uttered by the thief on the right of the Lord on the cross, with all his heart, made him enter into Paradise (Lk. 23: 42, 43).

The words of the prayer are not the important thing, but rather the feelings.

Is your prayer full of emotion, zeal, understanding and faith? Is it from a contrite heart with humbleness ? Is it full of feelings of love and longing to God? Does it have depth and meditation, or mere words you utter in the presence of God, coming from your mouth not from your heart?

Prayer is in fact lifting of the heart to God.

Prayer is not lifting of the hands or eyes upward, but rather lifting of the heart from all material and worldly matters to God wholly. See how the Lord rebukes the Jews, *"These people draw near to Me with their mouth, and honor Me with their lips, but their heart is far from Me"* (Mt. 15: 8), (Mk. 7: 6), (Isa. 29: 13).

In the light of the above words examine your prayer and try to feel the deep relationship between God and you.

You may see the difference even in the prayers of others.

You can discern whether their prayer is supplication from the heart and spiritual talk with God or mere reciting or keeping rhythm of hymns. You will be influenced by a person praying from his heart as if saying with the psalmist,
"With my whole heart I have sought You" (**Ps. 119: 10**).

This is exactly what God wants, *"And you will seek Me and find Me, when you search for Me with all your heart"* (Jer. 29: 13).

It is clearly evident then that prayer from the mouth is not a real prayer. That is why we sing in the Praise Hymn, "My heart and tongue give praise to the Holy One", beginning with the heart then the tongue.

❖ ❖ ❖

CHAPTER VIII

THOUGHTS

THOUGHTS

A Foreward:

Thoughts are the work of the mind, and might be good or evil according to one's condition

Meditation, for example, is a kind of good thoughts, likewise thoughts on God's love as the Holy Bible says, *"You shall love the Lord your God with all your heart, with all your soul, and with all your mind"* (Mt. 22: 37).

Among the good thoughts also is that related to Christ as St. Paul the apostle says, *"But we have the mind of the Christ"* (1 Cor. 2: 16).

On the other hand, there are wrong thoughts as those mentioned in the scriptures,

"The devising of foolishness is sin" (Prov. 24: 9), and, *"The thoughts of the wicked are an abomination to the Lord"* (Prov. 15: 26).

Now let us discuss here the mind and the thoughts.

The thoughts and the heart:

The mind is connected with the heart, it takes from it and gives it.

A sin of the mind might at the same time be a sin of the heart if it is coming out of the heart, as the Lord says, *"A good man out of the good treasure of his heart brings forth good; and an evil man out of the evil treasure of his heart brings forth evil"* (Lk. 6: 45).

And in the story of the flood it is written, *"Then the Lord saw that the wickedness of man was great in the earth, and that every intent of the thoughts of his heart was only evil continually"* (Gen. 6: 5).

The "thoughts of the heart" in the above verse mean the thoughts coming out of the heart.

It is not reasonable that a pure heart brings forth evil thoughts because, *"You will know them by their fruits ... every good tree bears good fruit, but a bad tree bears bad fruit"* (Mt. 7: 16, 17). And the Holy Bible commands us, first, to love the Lord our God with all our hearts; then, with all our minds (Mt. 22: 37). The heart comes first as it is written also,
*"Keep your heart with all diligence,
for out of it spring the issues of life"* (Prov. 4: 23).

So, you are required to keep your heart, to keep your mind, and to keep the line connecting the heart to the mind. But what is this connecting line?

The thoughts may come to you from outside, from other sources which we shall mention afterwards, if you accept such thoughts within you they will reach your heart.
The thoughts then will turn into feelings in the heart and into emotions.

An adulterous thought may turn into a lust of adultery, an angry thought may turn into angry excitement, and a thought of malice may turn into feelings of hatred. So, a sinful thought carries the sin to the heart. At the same time, the feelings of the heart turn into thoughts. Both exchange places and each becomes a cause and a result.

Wrong thoughts come out of the mind to the heart if one is lenient with the thought. And wrong thoughts come out of the heart to the mind if the heart is impure.

Another source of thoughts is senses:

The Senses:

The senses are the doors through which thoughts enter into the mind. What you see with your eyes you will think of, what you hear with your ears you will think of, whatever you touch, smell or even taste you will think of.

If you want to gain control over your thoughts, you should control your senses.

Do not let your senses unrestrained but be aware; for as the mind and heart exchange places, so also the thoughts and senses do. Your wrong thoughts may urge you to look, listen and touch. In the same way your wrong senses may bring you thoughts.

Another source of thoughts is environment and friendship:

Environment and friendship:

Those who you deal with may introduce to you good or bad thoughts, whether those be friends, acquaintances, neighbors, colleagues or relatives.

True indeed are the words said by the author:
Tell me who your friends are, and I tell you who you are.

Many thoughts are introduced through pressing on one's mind. You may hear today some thing which you do not believe, but if you hear it tomorrow with some conviction you will suspect. Afterwards if you are subject to more pressures you will accept it, and with more pressing you may believe in it and even spread it and react to it. This is part of what is called "brain washing".

Brain washing takes place when the mind is subjected for a long time to a consecutive pressing intellectual influence while keeping the mind away from any opposite scope for response or argument until one's thoughts are completely changed.

Thoughts may come also from the environment: from the public opinion, press, mass media and printed material.

Through reading, some became communists.

Some readings even bring forth lustful thoughts, and others bring philosophical thoughts. Other kinds of readings introduce spiritual or ascetic thoughts, or make you zealous for service or for certain beliefs.

Of the same effect like readings are radio, T.V., video and cassette. You are not alone in the world! Everything around you has its influence on you.

All this comes to the mind through thoughts from outside, not from the heart. The role of the heart in this case is its readiness to make use of such means.

Another source of thoughts is the generation of thoughts.

Generation of thoughts:

One thought brings forth another thought and generates suspicions and doubts and even dreams.

No thought is barren, especially with a fertile mind. You may have a certain thought from any source, you deal with it and it may bring forth many other thoughts which lie in the subconscious.

Subconscience is in fact another source of thoughts.

Subconscious:

The subconscious stores thoughts, images, events, desires and feelings. Thus it becomes a source of thoughts, dreams and suspicions.

The recorder or computer for example stores information that can be recalled whenever required. The brain is far dangerous because the information in it may come out against its will in the form of thoughts or dreams. This reminds us of some question addressed by some people;

Are sinful dreams considered a sin though they are involuntary?

The answer is that the sinful dreams might come from one's subconscious involuntarily, but they are not stored therein involuntarily. But if such dreams are mere fighting of the enemy, against one's will, one will resist and reject them in dream and might even wake up as if from an unbearable unpleasant thing.

Examine your dreams then, whether they are due to matters that settled in your mind as a result of lusts, images or thoughts. Such dreams are considered "quasi voluntary", because they are not due to a present will but to a previous will. However if your will at present rejects such lusts ... etc., you will resist them in dream.

Another source of thoughts is psychological causes;

Psychological causes:

A person who by nature is easily agitated and disturbed, is always subject to anxiety and agitation due to his own nature without any outer reason. Likewise, a person who is by nature apprehensive, is always attacked by fears. Similarly a suspicious person is always haunted and troubled by suspicions without any justifiable reason.

To be cured of all such thoughts, there must be a psychological treatment.

If one's nature is remedied, thoughts will also be remedied. So, a simple person is not usually haunted by doubts, and a calm gentle person cannot be fought by anxiety or fear.

According to one's nature, thoughts come to him. Someone might hear certain news and consider them very serious whereas they are not at all, but he imagined it according to his nature. Whereas someone else receives the same news very quietly and is not disturbed in mind by them.

Some person may be fought by despair and withdraws from a certain project, while another person in the same project does not withdraw and does not fall in despair but rather continues with a heart filled with hope.

If three persons see someone standing in the darkness; one of them may say he is either a thief or a murderer, the other says perhaps he has a date with a woman, and the third says he is praying. According to each one's nature his thoughts are formed.

Another source of thoughts is diabolic wars.

Diabolic wars:

The thoughts might not come from one's heart or nature, nor be due to environment or outer influences but might be wars cast into the mind by the devil.

But when are such wars considered sin? And when are not? And what is man's attitude towards them?

Thoughts Fighting The Mind (A)

There are two levels in the mind: An external level and a deep level.

Whatever matters you handle outwardly not giving much concern for, do not go deep into your mind and soon you will forget them.

Examples of these are news and trivial or casual talks in one's daily life. Such matters do not settle in the memory, nor in the heart and feelings. They are like vapor that appears for a little time then vanishes away (Jas. 4: 14).

On the contrary, matters taken deeply by the mind or internally and discussed by the mind for a long time, will enter into oneself and settle in the subconscious giving rise to other thoughts or leading to dreams, suspicions and feelings.

It depends then on one's way of thinking, not with regard to what happens to you or against you but with regard to your response to the thoughts.

Take for example distraction during prayers, and the relationship between this and the two levels in your mind; the external level and the deep level.

Why can there be distraction during prayer?

And what can be the cause, and the time at which distraction takes place?

A person may be distracted when he takes some matters deeply and lets them remain in his mind while praying, or when he remembers certain matters which he dealt with deeply in the past and they continue with him during praying. In such cases, two thoughts will be in his mind at the same time, that is prayer and distraction. Both might exchange places; one becomes in the external level and the other in the deep level. It depends on one's struggle and concentration on the words and meaning of the prayer, or one's submission to distraction. If a person is praying without understanding or not deeply, then his interior will accept distraction and he becomes like one not praying!!

On the other hand, a person who prays from the depth of his mind and heart, when he is fought by distraction he will refuse it immediately and it will find no place within him.

Thus, we say to those who are fought by distraction while praying:

Do not take all worldly matters deeply. Do not occupy your mind with what you see or hear by your senses. Do not let all this affect your minds, feelings and nerves, otherwise your mind will store them and present them to you during prayer, first externally, then, if acceptable, to the depths.

How perfect it will be if you arrange for a preliminary spiritual period before praying!

Through such a period, the mind will move from worldly matters to spiritual matters, because it is difficult for the mind to move suddenly from material involvement to pure spiritual thinking.

It is better that prayer be preceded by some spiritual songs or reading, by contemplation on a certain spiritual concept, or by some prostrations accompanied by quick supplications. Then a person would stand to pray and his mind empty of worldly matters and involvements. Such spiritual preparation is like giving incense on the altar before offering the holy sacrifice.

This reminds us of the story of St. John the short, who was seen by his disciple going around his cell thrice before going into it. When the disciple asked the saint about the reason for doing that, the saint answered, 'I was with some brothers and when they began to argue I left them. But their voices were still in my ears, so I preferred to go around my cell to remove away the voices from my ears before I enter'.
So careful the saint was with regard to the purity of his mind!

A person may be troubled if he is sensitive towards any matters.

A sensitive person is affected deeply by everything. This sensitivity implants the things within oneself and brings thoughts that press on a person and trouble him.
However, each one differs from the other in nature and mind.
If you face a problem, try to solve it finally, but if you found it difficult to be solved leave it for some time and do not be concerned about it. Put it in the hands of God who solves all problems and it will be solved by time.

Thoughts might dominate over a person when he thinks deeply without trying to find solutions; in other words, when he looks only at the troubles behind a problem without looking at possible solutions.

That is why some people -when faced with a problem- let the problem dominate over their mind, their feelings and their emotions. They think only of the problem, and speak only of it. It accompanies them while awake or asleep, while thinking or talking, it is within them. Such people cannot come out of the scope of the problem, their mind hands it to their heart and their heart hands it to their mind, and both heart and mind hand the problem to the nerves which carry it to the emotions and the tongue that talks of it with whom one meets. The problem thus remains within the mind for days and weeks and a person becomes involved in it all day long and dream of it by night.

Such thoughts might lead to body diseases such as high blood pressure, diabetes, ulcer nervous disease or mental disease. All this is due to excessive sensitivity which makes thoughts dominate.

On the contrary, a spiritual person has control over his thoughts and does not let them dominate over him.

Some people however do not like to let thoughts dominate over them and they try to remove them away but regrettably in a wrong way!!

When someone offends him, he says to himself I will not suppress anger within me, but I will deal with that person in the same way and harder. I will settle the matter with him. And the mind remains involved and instead of getting rid of the thoughts, they dominate over the person.

It is good to remove thoughts away, but in a spiritual practical way without suppression.

If thoughts are inflamed within you, do not cast fuel to them.

Thoughts can be settled first within, when the heart deals with them and when the outer causes are gotten rid of. One must not be lenient with a thought nor give it a chance to dominate over the mind.

Thoughts fighting the mind:

There is a question often addressed by some people:

Is every wrong thought occurring to us considered a sin?

The answer is: A thought might be an attack from the devil. It might also come to you from outside source or from wicked people. But if the thought comes from your own heart and your inner desires and lusts, it will then certainly be considered a sin.

When the sinful thought comes from outside, it will be judged according to your response to it, whether you accept it or not.

It will not be a sin if reject it, feel annoyed with it and dismiss it even though it presses on you and you refuse it from all your heart. You may even pray-while the thought is occupying your mind -asking God to save you from it. Up to this point the thought is considered an external war. When then may it be considered a sin?

A sin begins when the mind submits to it.

It increases when one responds to it, and accepts it, and when the will submits to it. At this point the mind will have opened its door to the sin voluntarily and begun to deal with it and perhaps responded to it emotionally letting it settle within.

It is thus well said in the Song, "*A garden enclosed is my sister, my spouse, a spring shut up, a fountain sealed*" (Song 4: 12).
She is shut up against all thoughts and guiles of the devil. The same was said by the psalmist, "*Praise the Lord, O Jerusalem ... For He has strengthened the bars of your gates*" (Ps. 147: 13).

Know, O brothers that fighting thoughts come weak at first and are on the surface of your mind.

It is therefore easy to dismiss thoughts at this point. But if you accept them, they will penetrate gradually into the depths. If you respond emotionally to them, they will go deeper and will stick to your will. And further if they reach the heart, they will mix with your feelings and the fight will be internal not external. Then the thoughts dominate and are difficult to dismiss.

How easy indeed for thoughts to enter the mind, and how difficult to dismiss them!

It is easy to accept a thought, and difficult to bring it out. Take for example doubts, lusts, revenge, greatness and vain glory, they are all thoughts that easily enter the mind and hardly come out. So, be aware not to let thoughts in.

Do not receive with welcome every thought that knocks at your door.

To an evil thought, you should say, *"Away with you, Satan!"* (Mt. 4: 10). Make the sign of the cross on yourself and dismiss the thought. Remember that if you open the doors of your mind to an evil thought, you will be a betrayer to God. And if you open the doors of your heart to it you will be the more a betrayer and will be like one dismissing the Holy Spirit dwelling within him (1 Cor. 3: 16).

Know that when a thought fights you from outside, your will is in this case more powerful and able to dismiss it. But when the thought creeps within, your will becomes weak and the devil gains power in his fight. He says: That person has opened the door for negotiation and we can deal with him and even make him join us completely!!

It is the same like a person offering a bribe to someone. If he finds him lenient, he will continue negotiation and attain his desire. But if he finds him firm from the beginning, he will not dare to continue. So, you have to reject a sinful thought from the very beginning. Do not deceive yourself, saying that you want to test the thought to know the result!! You certainly know to what it will lead you.

Dismiss the thought immediately before it penetrates deep within you. Dismiss it while it is still a little one, before it grows and gains power over you.

We remember here the words of the psalm, *"O daughter of Babylon ... Happy shall he be who takes and dashes your little ones against the rock"* (Ps. 137: 9). Although still little ones, they can be dashed and buried in the rock *"and the Rock was Christ"* (1 Cor. 10: 4). But if you let it grow, you may not be able to prevail over it. That is why the fathers said; Discipline your children before they discipline you. If you discipline a child, he will not dare disobey you when he grows up. Similarly, if you control a sinful thought while still a little one, you will be able to dismiss it before it grows.

Thoughts may dominate also because of a sinful lust in the heart not mere external war.

In such a case thoughts come from the heart, and being aroused by lusts, they press on the mind in such a way that the mind cannot escape the effect wishing to turn the thought into action. The sin will have reigned over the heart, the feelings and over the mind. A person then will *"of the evil treasure of his heart bring forth evil"* (Lk. 6: 45).

Certainly, repentance is needed to save the heart from its lusts so that it might stop to be a source of evil thoughts. A renewal of the mind is also needed as the apostle says, *"be transformed by the renewing of your mind"* (Rom. 12: 2).

But the renewing of the mind requires positive action and not mere passive struggling against thoughts.

Thoughts Fighting The Mind (B)

Thoughts which fight the mind come either from outside or from within as we have previously said.

Fights from outside are like those that occurred to our mother Eve.

Eve was a simple, calm and innocent woman. Thoughts of doubt came to her from outside, from the serpent when it said to her, *"Has God indeed said you shall not eat of every tree of the garden? ... You will not surely die. For God knows that in the day you eat of it your eyes will be opened, and you will be like God, knowing good and evil"* (Gen. 3: 1-5).

Such thought, which came to Eve from outside, troubled her because she accepted it.

That thought moved to the senses, then to the heart.

When the thought moved to the senses, Eve saw the tree differently and found that *"the tree was good for food, that it was pleasant to the eyes, and a tree desirable to make one wise"* (Gen. 2: 6). The heart changed within, and the senses without. The mind lost its purity and led the will away from God.

As for you, resist any sinful thought that might occure to you.

There is a means of resistance for every thought. Some thoughts flee if faced by one or more verses, others by certain emotions.

Take for example the thought of pride or vain glory:

This thought can be resisted by reminding yourself of your sins so this thought of pride gets ashamed. You can also remind yourself of the high spiritual levels attained by saints that you may feel you are nothing compared to them. Say to yourself: If I obeyed this thought, the grace will quit me and I will fall in many sins as the scriptures say, *"Pride goes before destruction. And a haughty spirit before a fall"* (Prov. 16: 18).

Or say: This achievement which I pride myself on is not my work but God's work through me. If I ascribe it to myself, God will not work with me lest I fall in pride, and then I will fail to do any good thing!!

It is not for my benefit.

When you remember the work of grace within you, pride will quit you, and by this and other means you will get rid of such thoughts.

Some saints were especialized in dealing with thoughts. They guided others to the means of fighting thoughts. Among those is St. Evagrius who compiled articles on the wars of thoughts and the means of resisting them.

One way of resisting thoughts is the use of a verse from the Holy Bible for each thought.

When you are fought with thoughts of anger for example, face them with the words, *"for the wrath of man does not produce the righteousness of God"* (Jas. 1: 20).

If you are fought with thoughts of adultery, say with Joseph the righteous, *"How then can I do this great wickedness, and sin against God?"* (Gen. 39: 9). Or remember the words of St. Paul the apostle, *"Do not be deceived. Neither fornicators nor idolaters, nor adulterers, nor homosexuals, nor sodomites, nor thieves ... will inherit the Kingdom of God"* (1 Cor. 6: 9, 10).

If you are fought with the love of the world, remember the words of St. James the apostle, *"friendship with the world is enmity with God"* (Jas. 4: 4), and the words of St. John the apostle, *"Do not love the world or the things in the world. If anyone loves the world, the love of the Father is not in him*"(1 Jn. 2: 15).

There is a verse for every thought that can dismiss it. You just have to learn the verses with which you can reject the thoughts that fight you.

Our saintly fathers had experience in fighting thoughts

It is good to remember this when we read their stories to benefit from their experience. But put in mind that you have, at least, to reject any evil thought and dismiss it immediately. Keep your doors shut according to the teaching of the Holy Bible. You have also to be firm against it and remember how Job the righteous -when his wife introduced to him a wrong thought- replied her firmly and rebuked her, saying *"You speak as one of the foolish women speaks"* (Job 2: 10). In this way he silenced her with power. You also, if any wrong thought occurs to you, silence it. Do not allow yourself to respond to it. Say to yourself the words of Job (Job 2: 10).

There are two ways by which you can get rid of the wars of thoughts, namely; purity of the heart and mind and occupation of the heart and mind.

Occupation of the mind:

It is a protective positive way by which one can get rid of thoughts before they come.

If our mind is occupied with God, we shall attain His love. And when God's love settles deep in our hearts, our nature will become incapable of accepting thoughts from the enemy.

This is like a healthy person, no microbe can fight him and prevail. Likewise, a person who has immunity against a certain disease, that disease will never attack him because it has no place within him.

A person must not leave himself susceptible to diseases then try to cure them!! One should seek the means to prevent disease attacks.

Likewise, a spiritual person can immunize himself against evil thoughts by filling his heart and mind with the love of God and the love of good. We say to him:

Occupy your mind before the devil comes to occupy it.

Occupy you mind with good thoughts, with contemplation and spiritual readings before the enemy of good introduces to you his thoughts. When a person has a residence and leaves it empty, wicked people might occupy it. In this case it might be difficult to get them out of it. But if the house has lights and furniture in every place, no one can enter it by force, for he will be afraid of the inhabitants and will apprehend risk.

If your mind is busy, the devil will know that you will not welcome him and will leave you even for a while.

And if your mind is continually busy, he will find no way to enter into you. Not only spiritual involvement is useful but also scientific occupation, involvement in work, in various activities, and even in sports, arts or manual work.

Therefore clever students who always occupy their minds with their study have no time for sinful thoughts, as the saying goes,

The mind of the lazy is a lab for the devil.

On the contrary, the students who neglect their study are more susceptible to sinful thoughts because their minds are empty and the devil can settle there.

So, occupy your mind with useful things, whether useful to your spirituality and eternal life, to your knowledge, or to your service. Occupy your mind with readings and contemplations, in short, with any thing of benefit.

If you are idle your mind not busy, it will be easy for the devil to say to you: May I come and amuse you?

The devil may say to you: I have some stories to tell you. I have some ideas for you since you have nothing to think of.

Then he will take you from one subject to another till you are completely under his control or at least some time is wasted in nonsense.

Our saintly fathers trained themselves to pray permanently or to repeat the prayer "O Lord Jesus Christ" hundreds or thousands of times. Their minds used to be occupied with this prayer that they repeated it automatically.

Even if the saint was silent, his mind would be occupied with this prayer without any effort on his behalf to force the mind to repeat it. The same applies to occupying the mind with verses or stories from the Holy Bible, with contemplation on a spiritual subject, or with stories of saints.

When you go out of your home, do not leave your mind empty without arranging something to think of on your way.

Do not leave it for meetings, sights or talks to impose themselves on you introducing a certain thought and a fuel to kindle your mind. How easy it is for you when leaving home to take a verse or psalm, a spiritual subject, or a certain deep idea to nourish your mind on the way.

In the morning, read a chapter of the Holy Bible and choose part of it to contemplate on. Or take a psalm and memorize it. So, when any thought attacks you, it will find you busy and your doors shut.

The mind cannot think of two subjects at the same time and be occupied with them equally

If you think deeply on some useful matter, any other thought will float to the surface of your mind and will quickly vanish, seeing you are not interested in it nor have time for it. Again, if you want to protect yourself from the fights of thoughts, you have to do the following:

Present to your mind spiritual food before the world presents to it bad food
Keep a spiritual notebook where you can record some thoughts that had a good influence on you.

You can read, from time to time, what you have recorded in it and ruminate on it as the camel does on food previously stored by it. Then contemplate on such beautiful thoughts and add to them other thoughts of benefit.

But if your mind is filled with past sinful thoughts, try to clean your mind from them by neglecting them or replacing them by others.

Do not occupy your mind with trivial thoughts. They might be neither good nor bad, but they may develop and you lose control over them.
[This point is expounded in our book entitled "Life of Repentance & Purity", in the chapter on "Purity of the Mind"]

Try to clean your heart within, because a pure heart cannot bring forth sinful thoughts

See what the Lord says in this regard, "*A good tree cannot bear bad fruit, nor can a bad tree bear good fruit*" (Mt. 7: 18).

CHAPTER IX

THE HUMAN SPIRIT

THE HUMAN SPIRIT
And Its Relationship With The Holy Spirit

To speak about spiritual life or life in the Spirit we should deal with two important matters; namely, the human soul and God's Holy Spirit with regard to His work in the human spirit.

The human spirit:

In the Epistle to the Romans, St. Paul the apostle says,
"There is therefore now no condemnation to those who are in Christ Jesus, who do not walk according to the flesh, but according to the Spirit" (Rom. 8: 1). Here the apostle emphasizes behavior according to the spirit. But to behave according to the Spirit, a person must strengthen his spirit so that it might win over the flesh and over the material, the sin and the world.

So, St. Paul says in the same chapter, *"For those who live according to the flesh set their minds on the things of the flesh, but those who live according to the Spirit, the things of the Spirit. For to be carnally minded is death, but to be spiritually minded is life and peace"* (Rom. 8: 5, 6).

The power of the Spirit appears even in the unbelievers. The Hindus have deep spiritual exercises by which they strengthen and give power to their human spirits.

The Yoga groups gain power in spirit through their exercises notwithstanding the work of the Holy Spirit. Hence, many people, even non Christians who do not believe in the Holy Spirit and who are not anointed with the Holy Myron, can have powerful human spirits and can lead a good life far from the evil lusts of the world whatever their faith might be.

But a believer has two things to do: To strengthen his human spirit, and to have communion with the Holy Spirit. No doubt a believer who attains this is in a level much higher than that of an unbeliever.

The communion of the Holy Spirit:

When the human spirit has communion with the Holy Spirit, it is under two obligations: The first is positive, and the second is passive.

The passive aspect is that the human soul has to keep away from quenching the Spirit, grieving the Spirit, resisting the Spirit or blaspheming against the Spirit.

The Holy Bible mentions all this, saying,

"Do not quench the Spirit" (1 Thess. 5: 19);

"And do not grieve the Holy Spirit of God, by whom you were sealed" (Eph. 4: 30);

And St. Stephen the first deacon said to the Jews *"You stiff-necked ... You always resist the Holy Spirit; as your fathers did, so do you"* (Acts 7: 51).

And the Lord Christ mentioned the blasphemy against the Holy Spirit (Mt. 12: 31).

As for the positive side of the relationship with the Holy Spirit, it starts with the birth from the Spirit.

As the Lord said, *"that which is born of the Spirit is spirit"* (Jn. 3: 6); *"unless one is born of water and the Spirit, he cannot enter the kingdom of God"* (Jn. 3: 5). Of course man is born of the Spirit in the baptism.

The second relationship with the Spirit is in the holy anointment

As St. John the apostle said, *"But you have an anointing from the Holy One"* (1 Jn. 2: 20, 27). It is the holy anointment in the Sacrament of the Holy Myron (the chrismation).

By this anointment the body becomes a temple of the Holy Spirit.

St. Paul the apostle said about this, *"Do you not know that you are the temple of God and that the Spirit of God dwells in you?"* (1 Cor. 3: 16).

A third point on the relationship with the Holy Spirit is the communion with the Spirit.

St. Paul says, in the final blessing, *"The grace of the Lord Jesus Christ, and the love of God, and the communion of the Holy Spirit be with you all."* (2 Cor. 13: 14). It is a communion between God's Holy Spirit and man's spirit; a communion of work, in which God's Spirit works with you, in you, and through you.

However, man's spirit should respond to the work of the Holy Spirit.

In this way, there will be a communion with the Holy Spirit. As for blasphemy against the Holy Spirit, it means complete rejection of the work of the Spirit, for the whole life, by which man does not repent because he cannot repent without the work of the Spirit in him. And not repenting, one's sins will not be forgiven.

A fourth point is that man grows in such communion with the Spirit till he perfects the commandment:

"Be filled with the Spirit" (Eph. 5: 18).

In other translations *"Let God's Spirit fill you"*.

A fifth point: By having this communion with the Spirit, and by being filled with the Spirit, a person attains an important thing i.e. the fruit of the Spirit which St. Paul mentioned in his epistle to the Galatians (Gal. 5: 22, 23). This fruit of the Spirit is due both to the work of God's Spirit within man and to man's response to this work in communion with the Spirit.

It is an integrated spiritual discipline; for when a person walks according to the Spirit, in continual communion with God's Spirit, he will certainly attain a clear benefit, that is:

The sixth point: Fervence of the spirit, as the apostle said, *"Be ... , fervent in spirit"* **(Rom. 12: 11).**

Since our God *"is a consuming fire"* (Heb. 12: 29), it is natural that a person whose spirit lives in communion with God's Spirit will certainly be fervent in spirit. And when he gets away from the Spirit, his spirit will become luke warm.

That is why God's Spirit descended on the disciples on the Day of Pentecost in tongues *"as of fire"* (Acts 2: 3).

And as the angels are spiritual beings, or spirits, it is said of the disciples in the psalm, *"Who makes His angels spirits, His ministers a flame of fire"* (Ps. 104: 4).

A spiritual person is distinguished by his fervence.

His prayers are very fervent, inflamed with the divine love. A fervent prayer is accompanied by tears, with humiliation and strong faith, and is perhaps distinguished with its words and expressions.

An example of such a fervent prayer is the prayer of the believers for the apostle, by which the place where they were assembled together was shaken (Acts 4: 31).

The spirituality of a person who is fervent in spirit appears in his fervent service.

His service is inflamed with zealous fire of which the psalmist said *"Zeal for Your house has eaten me"* (Ps. 69: 9). It is an enthusiastic powerful service unlike unspiritual service which is sluggish and weak, mere routine without influence.

Spiritual fervence appears also in one's private life:

St. John the beloved says in the beginning of his revelation *"I was in the Spirit on the Lord's Day"* (Rev. 1: 10). It means that he was in a certain spiritual condition.

The life of the Spirit is evident in the strong divine life; for love is described as fire, as in the Song of Songs, *"Many waters cannot quench love, nor can the floods drown it"* (Song 8: 7). Love is like a fire whether it is love of God, of people, of church or of service.

The work of the Spirit in man gives him fervence. But some people misunderstand gentleness as if a gentle person has no fervence or liveliness!

A seventh point is that if a person walks according to the Spirit and enjoys the dwelling of God's Spirit in him, he will enjoy what is called the authority of the Spirit or the power of the Spirit.

Such a person will have power over his own body and power over the devils as the disciples were given by the Lord, *"He gave them power over unclean spirits to cast them out"* (Mt. 10: 1). The Lord said to them, *"Behold, I give you the authority to trample on serpents and scorpions, and over all the power of the enemy"* (Lk. 10: 19). The Spirit in such a case will have influence even on others. Thus the word gains power and penetrates into the mind and the heart influencing people.

A person who reveres and aws his father, it is because the spirit of his father and the authority of the law, the commandment and nature have power over him. Whereas a person whose body and spirit are still fighting *"and these are contrary to one another"* (Gal. 5: 17) and the spirit is sometimes defeated, such a person has lost power over his spirit. When the spirit overcomes, it will have power. This power made the devils tremble before some saints.

The eighth point is that a person who lives according to the Spirit is a powerful person who has no fear.

Such a person has inner power not dreading any external thing, unlike those who are afraid; their spirits have no power and they are cowardly. The Book of the Revelation classifies them at the top of those who will perish, *"But the cowardly, unbelieving, abominable, murderers, sexually immoral, sorcerers, idolaters, and all liars shall have their part in the lake which burns with fire and brimstone"* (Rev. 21: 8). How strange that the cowardly are far from God's Spirit who is the source of power, as the Lord said *"But you shall receive power when the Holy Spirit has come upon you; and you shall be witnesses to Me"* (Acts 1: 8).

A person who receives power from God's Spirit will serve with power and will speak with power. Thus the early church was powerful and through it the kingdom of God came powerfully. The weakness of the ministers is that they serve much but without power, they are very active but not with the power of the Spirit!!

The Spirit and Care for it

St. Paul the apostle says, *"For those who live according to the flesh set their minds on the things of the flesh, but those who live according to the Spirit, the things of the Spirit. For to be carnally minded is death, but to be spiritually minded is life and peace"* (Rom. 8: 5, 6).

If so, how should you care for your spirit?

See how you care for your body and whether you do care for the spirit to the same extent.

Nourishing the spirit:

* You nourish your body everyday, nay, thrice a day, with enough quantities as necessary.

But do you give your spirit its nourishment every day?

You give your body all the necessary elements and kinds of food: calcium for building the bones, iron for building the blood, protein for building the tissues, sugar and carbohydrates to give the necessary energy, and vitamins and various elements as well. But do you give your spirit all kinds of nourishment it needs?

The spirit needs to be nourished with spiritual readings, spiritual contemplation, liturgies and spiritual meetings, hymns and songs, spiritual thoughts, spiritual influence, and spiritual companionship.

Do you actually provide it with all this for its benefit and power?

* You give the body rest, and the spirit also needs quietude and spiritual retreat. Do you provide it with this? Do you give it rest through faith and inner peace?

* When the body is ill, you go to the physicians and obey their commands and take the necessary medicine. The spirit also, when not well, needs spiritual physicians i.e. the spiritual fathers and guides whom you should obey and follow the remedy they prescribe.

In medical treatment, protection is better than treatment.

In spiritual treatment, likewise, you should avoid whatever weakens your spirit, and avoid all causes leading to sin. Avoid evil company that corrupts good habits (1 Cor. 15: 33); for *"Blessed is the man who walks not in the counsel of the ungodly, nor stands in the path of sinners, nor sits in the seat of the scornful"* (Ps. 1: 1). Thus the spirit gets power when it keeps away from environment that weakens or destroys it.

All these are normal means, how better rather will be the condition of the spirit if it is God's Spirit that works in it and leads it. In this case the spirit will have a touch of beauty which is called "the ornament of the spirit".

The ornament of the spirit:

It is so strange that a person stands before the mirror before going out to look at himself, to be sure of being handsome, pleasant and pretty, whereas he does not care for his spirit and its beauty and adornment. What then can be the ornament of the spirit?

A spirit is ornamented with virtues as St. Peter the apostle said, *"ornament of a gentle and quiet spirit"* **(1 Pet. 3: 4).**

The heavenly Jerusalem that represents the church in the coming world is described in the Revelation as, *"a bride adorned for her husband"* (Rev. 21: 2). And the Song of Songs describes the church in general, or the human spirit in particular, as *" perfumed with myrrh and frankincense, with all the merchant's fragrant powders "* (Song 3: 6). It is like that in the eyes of God as well as in the eyes of the people. They see it adorned with meekness, delicacy, humbleness and gentleness. Are you sure that your spirit has all this before you go out and before you meet others so that you might not stumble anyone, but people would rather see you with your spiritual adornment, *"see your good works and glorify your Father in heaven"* (Mt. 5: 16).

Of this spiritual adornment we sing in the Praise Hymn, saying, [You adorned our souls, O Moses the Prophet, with the honor of the Dome you adorned.]

With such adornment the spirit is beautified when meeting the Lord in heaven. One leaves the body dead in the bed while the spirit ascends to God perfumed with the pleasant aroma of

Christ as holy burnt offering from which the Lord smells soothing aroma (Gen. 8).

A spirit adorned with virtues is indeed God's image on earth.

In this beautiful image God created us in the beginning with a spirit adorned with innocence and simplicity as seen in Adam and Eve, a spirit that knew no evil at all. The Song of Songs describes this spirit as, *"fair as the moon, clear as the sun"* (Song 6: 10).

When St. John the beloved wrote his revelation he said:

I was in the Spirit:

St. John said, *"I was in the Spirit on the Lord's Day"*
What does it mean that he was in the Spirit?
If we contemplate on these words, we find that they refer to a spiritual status which reminds us of the words of St. Paul the apostle when he ascended to the third heaven, for he said, *"whether in the body I do not know, or whether out of the body I do not know, God knows"* (2 Cor. 12: 2).

It is the condition of one in the Spirit, where the Spirit works solely and the body is not working at all with the Spirit. Even the senses which are watching and hearing the inexpressible words in the vision (2 Cor. 12: 4) are not the senses of the body but of the Spirit. The bodily look and utterance are out of this scope, they cannot interfere in things above them.

It is the condition or utterance of *"the man whose eyes are opened ... who hears the words of God, who sees the vision of the Almighty"* (Num. 24: 3-5).

This reminds us of the prayer of Elisha the prophet for his servant Gehazi that the Lord open his eyes that he might see (2 Kgs. 6: 17).

It reminds us also of the words of the Lord to His holy disciples, *"But blessed are your eyes for they see"* (Mt. 13: 16). No doubt the Lord was not speaking about bodily eyes, but about the spirit's vision. With the same meaning He said *"and (blessed are) your ears for they hear"*.

In eternity we shall see what the eye had not seen nor the ear heard (1 Cor. 2: 9) because such things are more sublime than the bodily senses and beyond their comprehensibility.

We only see these things in the Spirit, with the Spirit.

May God give us such spiritual vision that we may be open-eyed! But we should, at least, give God's Spirit chance to work within us and have communion with the Spirit.

Communion of the Spirit:

By this we mean that our spirits live in continual communion with God's Spirit. Of this communion St. Paul the apostle says, *"the communion of the Holy Spirit be with you all"* (2 Cor. 13: 14). By this communion all our life becomes spiritual life, our words become spiritual words, our love to people becomes spiritual love, our behavior becomes spiritual, and when we behave wisely, it will be spiritual wisdom coming down from the Father of lights.

Thus will the words of the apostle apply to us,

"*There is therefore now no condemnation to those who are in Christ Jesus, who do not walk according to the flesh, but according to the Spirit*" (**Rom. 8: 1**)

Those who are in Christ Jesus are those who can do nothing without Him (Jn. 15: 5), of whom the Lord said, "*that ... I (be) in them*" (Jn. 17: 26). The more those grow in the Spirit, the more they will be able to say with St. Paul the apostle, "*it is no longer I who live, but Christ lives in me*" (Gal. 2: 20). For so long as it is Christ that lives in them, there will be no condemnation to them. He will work in them because He lives in them. In this position you seem as if saying to the Lord:

For what will you condemn me, O Lord, since I did nothing on my own!! All things were made through You, and without You nothing was made that was made.

These words were said about creation in the beginning, but they may be similarly said about spiritual life and your communion with God and with His Spirit because "*if anyone is in Christ, he is a new creation*" (2 Cor. 5: 17).

This life to which there is no condemnation is the life of complete continual submission to God's Spirit.

It is not a life with temporary communion with the Holy Spirit, but with complete communion so as the Spirit takes part in every work you do and in every word you utter as the Lord said, "*for it is not you who speak, but the Spirit of your Father who speaks in you*" (Mt. 10: 20).

How beautiful it is if God's Spirit takes part with you in everything without any separation between Him and you. He dwells in you and you become a temple for Him (1 Cor. 3: 16), and you become a tool in His hands by which He does whatever He wants.

So becoming, you will also have the awe of the spirit.

The awe of the spirit:

Your spirit loses its esteem when it submits to the devil and gives him place to work in it and direct it. But a spirit that stands firm in front of the devil, leaning on her beloved (Song 8: 5), this spirit will have awe before the devil. It is the spirit of one having God's promise, *"A thousand may fall at your side, and ten thousand at your right hand, but it shall not come near you"* (Ps. 91: 7).

In front of such people, the devils cry out in fear and weakness.

The devils tried to find for themselves a way into them but failed, so they became afraid and not able to come near to them. They fear to see God's image in them.

This awe of the spirit is not due to a feeling of greatness or pride, but because of humbleness.

The devil confessed this to St. Macarius the great, saying to him, 'By your humbleness you defeat us'. It is because the devils see in a humble person the image of the humble God, who in His incarnation *"made Himself of no reputation, taking the form of a servant"* (Phil. 2: 7).

Humbleness was the garment for the divinity when He became incarnate for our salvation.

The spirits before which the devils feel awe, are the spirits that struggled and won.

The devils cannot tempt or deceive such spirits not even forcibly because they are spirits that do not submit to the adversary, not even in little slips. They are faithful to their Creator, do not betray Him but walk circumspectly (Eph. 5: 15). These spirits do not want anything from the devil, nor have any desire whatsoever with him. They are great indeed!

Great spirits:

These spirits are great in their love, in their virtuousness, and in their power and capability. They are great in their spirituality. They do not stop at the point of repentance and struggle, but grow continually in the life of righteousness till they attain holiness. Then they grow in holiness seeking perfection according to the Lord's commandment, *"Therefore you shall be perfect, just as your Father in heaven is perfect"* (Mt. 5: 48).

Such spirits do not seek only their own salvation but also the salvation of those who hear them (1 Tim. 4:16). They build the kingdom.

Some great spirits are not confined to serving God here on earth, but after they leave the body and ascend to heaven, are entrusted by God to carry out some services on earth again.

God may delegate some spirits to save His children in the world, or to carry out a certain task, such as the spirit of St. George, of St. Mina or the spirits of some martyrs and saints whose intercession we ask for. Their lives did not end by death; they are still working. These great spirits differ from the weak little spirits that still struggle against the body, and repent for few days then return to sin and to the habits to which they submit in weakness.

Great spirits are also great in their knowledge, and have wisdom and discernment.

God has endowed these spirits with understanding and intelligence. They are thus able to guide and lead others. The wisdom they have is not due to a human hand, but it is a gift of the Spirit (1 Cor. 12).

In implementing God's commandments, these spirits walk according to the Spirit not to the letter (2 Cor. 3: 6).

The Spirit ... Not the Letter

St. Paul the apostle concentrates on two phrases:
"Walk according to the Spirit" and *"spiritually minded"* (Rom. 8: 1, 6).

No doubt those who are spiritually minded are keen about following the spirit of the commandment not the letter thereof.

This is because *"the letter kills, but the Spirit gives life"* (2 Cor. 3: 6). Therefore, as the apostle says in the same verse " ... *made us sufficient as ministers of the new convenient, not of the letter but of the Spirit"*.

A person who walks according to the letter is a Pharisee or a lawyer.
He is like the Jews in their attitude regarding the Sabbath commandment!

The Pharisees were holding to the letter as in the case of the Sabbath commandment. When the Lord opened the eyes of the born blind on Saturday, they said, *"This Man is not from God, because He does not keep the Sabbath"* (Jn. 9: 16), and said to the man who was blind, *"Give God the glory! We know that this Man is a sinner"* (Jn. 9: 24).

And when the Lord healed the man at the Pool of Bethesda who had been sick for 38 years, the Jews sought to kill Him because He had done these things on the Sabbath (Jn. 5: 16).

It is the letter that kills because it implies lack of understanding of the spirituality of the commandment.

How then can one walk in the Spirit?

Let us contemplate on some virtues and see how we can behave according to them:

Fasting, for example, how can it be spiritual?

Fasting

Many of those who fast think that fasting is just vegetarian food. They prepare for themselves very delicious vegetarian food increasing its richness by adding various expensive rare kind of foodstuff!! They search for vegetarian fat, vegetarian cheese, vegetarian milk, vegetarian chocolate ... etc., and forget what Daniel the prophet said about his fasting,

"I, Daniel, was mourning three full weeks. I ate no pleasant food, no meat or wine came into my mouth, nor did I anoint myself at all" (Da. 10: 2, 3).

I want to concentrate here on the words *"I ate no pleasant food"*, because if a person eats delicious pleasant food while fasting, how will he be able to control the desires of his body so long as he give his body whatever food it desires?

How then shall the spirit take part with the body in fasting so that our fasting might not be mere fasting of the body in a literal way far from spirituality?

In a spiritual fasting, the spirit is ascetic and above the level of the material and the food of the body. During fasting we give the spirit its spiritual nutrition and the chance to have control over the body [see my book: Spirituality of Fasting].

Another point is metanias (prostration)

Metanias:

Metania means prostration. But what does this signify?

Prostration is not mere bowing of the body, but also bowing of the spirit with the body.

Therefore the psalmist said, *"But as for me, I will come into Your house in the multitude of Your mercy. In fear of You I will worship toward Your holy temple"* (Ps. 5: 7). The word *"In fear of You"* signifies humbleness of the spirit while prostrating. And the phrase *"I will come into Your house in the multitude of Your mercy"* signifies the feeling that one is not deserving. That is why the deacon cries out in the Holy Mass.
[**Worship God in fear and trembling**]

The spiritual feelings accompany the movement of the body.
Sometimes you apologize to someone and prostrate yourself before him but he does not accept it well. It is because he feels that you do it as a bodily action without spirit.

You might exclaim then, saying: what shall I do for him more than that? I have prostrated myself and bowed with my head even to the ground!!

O brother, it is your spirit that should bow. Do not hold to the letter of prostration not the spirit.

Hence David the prophet said,

"My soul clings to the dust" (Ps. 119: 25).

He did not say my head clings to the dust.

Prayer:

Literally speaking, prayer is talk with God. Spiritually speaking, it is attachment of one's spirit to God's spirit.

A person may pray, or thinks that he is praying but without such attachment between him and God!!

So, God reprimanded the Jews, saying, *"These people draw near to Me with their mouths and honor Me with their lips, but have removed their hearts far from Me"* (Isa. 29: 13) (Mt. 15: 8).It is unacceptable prayer because God wants the heart.

Do you think that you are praying because you move your lips before God?!

You might be doing so without understanding, without spirit or emotions, without love, contrition or humbleness!!

Are you just satisfying your conscience with regard to prayer? Can you be satisfied with such a prayer? Or you should rather pray with your spirit, and with your mind, with understanding of every word you say in your prayer.

St. Isaac truly said about such prayer:

Say to yourself I do not stand before God to count the words.

Some people are concerned about extending their prayer for a long time even without understanding, or they recite a big number of psalms quickly without contemplating on them or comprehending the meaning while praying!!

The psalms are all spiritual, but they are confined to the letter.

They do the same with the praise hymns of the psalmody and many other hymns; they utter the words very quickly without comprehending the meaning. They are interested in the letter not the spirit. What avails to them is to feel that they fulfilled their obligation with regard to prayer and their conscience is thus satisfied. But in fact such a prayer did not ascend before God because there was no attachment. Neither the spirit not the heart did take part in it. How beautiful are the words of St. Paul the apostle,

"I will pray with the spirit, and I will also pray with the understanding.

I will sing with the spirit, and I will also sing with the understanding" (1 Cor. 14: 15).

The kiss:

We hear in the Holy Mass the words "Kiss each other with a holy kiss" The kiss is a deep expression of love, and to be holy means that it should be pure without hypocrisy.

Then each one greets the other beside him as a symbol of having peace with all people. But do we do this outwardly or literally while there is no peace within our hearts with others?!

Judas Iscariot kissed the Lord Christ.

But it was a literal kiss not with the spirit, and the letter kills. It was an outward action of love but concealed betrayal behind it. That is why the church prohibits kissing from the Wednesday of the Pasion Week till the end of the week as a rejection of the treacherous kiss of Judas.

You also, when you meet any one, you begin with greeting

Is this greeting merely literal? Or is it true greeting in the spiritual sense? So many are our words, greetings and courtesy but they are merely literal, not with spirit!

Would we refrain then from showing courtesy? Nay.

We should rather add to them the spirit and the truth to show love, compassion, good relationship and respect to people. We should do this from all our hearts so that it might be apparent in our features and looks, not according to the letter but to the Spirit.

Giving:

Giving, according to the Spirit, is an expression of love and heart participation in the needs of the people and the church.

However, some people take it literally: just giving!! So they give even forcibly without love!

Those people forget the words of the apostle, *"God loves a cheerful giver"* (2 Cor. 9: 7). Giving begins from the heart, not only from the hand. A spiritual giver rejoices when he gives because he feels that he takes part in making someone happy or obtains the blessing of participating in providing the church needs.

Yet some people behave as if making up accounts with God!!

They just pay the tithes (if they ever do)!! And they are very careful that giving does not exceed the tithes. They might even deduct from the tithes what they are obliged to give to their relatives and acquaintances, or what they are forced to pay on certain occasions for some projects or services!

It is because the heart is not taking part in giving, nor the spirit!

When the spirit takes part we do not feel elevated above the poor to whom we give because we know that they receive from God not from us. He gave us that which we give them.
Giving by force, or without love, is giving without spirit.
Service:

We sometimes take service literally or formally, thinking we are participating in the church service though we do not go into the spirit of the service. Even literally speaking, we forget the literal meaning of the word "server".

We forget the humbleness necessary fro service.

The mind takes part in the service with the knowledge it has, and the body takes part with its activity, while the spirit does not take part! Thus, the service becomes a chance for showing off, and is mixed with love of domination, influence, and competition among the servers, a matter which is not consistent at all with the word "server". It seems as if we concentrate in

our service on ourselves not on the kingdom of Christ as St. John the Baptist said,
"He must increase, but I must decrease" (**Jn. 3: 30**).

Thus, service becomes mere information given by the Sunday Schools teacher, or mere management and financial work carried out by the Church Board and committees or mere activities carried out by the church authorities, while in all this we forget the spirit of service and our spirits do not take part in the service!!

The Sabbath:

It is the Lord Day (now Sunday). To keep the Sabbath literally means not to do any work in it (Ex. 20: 10).

But according to the Spirit, it is a Sabbath for the Lord, or a rest for the Lord in which the Lord takes rest with you and His children also take rest.

It is the Lord's Day, so if you do good in it, you will have done what gives rest to the Lord and to the people. Thus it becomes a Sabbath; a rest.

That is what the Lord Christ taught us; that we can do good on the Sabbath, since doing good gives people rest. It is the spirit of the commandment. On the other hand, doing no work at all might give rest to the body not to the spirit nor to the people whom you did not serve by refraining completely from working!

Rituals:

Are you aware of the spirituality of every church ritual? Do you take part in it with your spirit?

Do you know that when the priest carries the gospel above his head and turns around the altar, this refers to the spreading of the gospel all over the world? Do you pray for this to be realized?

And when the deacon carries a candle while the gospel is being read, it refers to the words of the psalmist, *"Your word is a lamp to my feet and a light to my path"* (Ps. 119: 105). Do you accept the words of the gospel to enlighten your mind, your heart, and your conscience?

When the high priest lifts his crown from over his head in awe and respect for the word of the gospel, do you also feel the same awe, and your spirit takes part in the same ritual?

Does your spirit take part in the rituals expressed by the priest's movements and work in the church?

If you do so, your spirit -not only your senses- will be taking part in the Holy Mass and all liturgies, because it is the spirit that gives life (2 Cor. 3: 6).

The same applies to feasts.

Do you rejoice only because the fasting ended, or you enter into the spirituality of the feast? For example in the Nativity, you should rejoice in the birth of the Lord Christ because it is the beginning of the history of salvation implying humbleness and love. You should rejoice in the Resurrection because it represents victory over death, a start point of resurrection of all people and opening of Paradise. Let all this be in your heart and emotions.

The Creed:

Do you take the creed literally as mere theological matters and beliefs that give place to arguments with other denominations?

With regard to baptism, for example, do your spirit go deep into the phrase, *"buried with Him in baptism"* (Col. 2: 12), being aware that it is death and life with the Lord Christ (Rom. 6: 4, 8)? Are you aware that being buried thus, our old man is crucified and raised a new man in the newness of life (Rom. 6: 6, 4)?

Ask yourself whether "the old man" still exists in your life, and what is the new life that you have acquired in baptism? Did you put on Christ in baptism as the apostle said (Gal. 3: 27)? In other words, did you put on His righteousness and His divine image in which He came? In this way you will have entered into the spirit of baptism. The same applies to other beliefs.

Birth from God, for example, is it, literally speaking, mere belief subject to argument as to the time when a Christian is being born of God?

Or you go into the depth of this belief remembering the words of the apostle, *"Whoever has been born of God does not sin ... and he cannot sin, because he has been born of God"* (1

Jn. 3: 9), and also, " ... *he who has been born of God keeps himself, and the wicked one does not touch him*" (1 Jn. 5: 18).

In this way, whenever you pray the Lord's prayer and say "Our Father" you will feel remorse. You will say to the Lord, "*I am no longer worthy to be called Your son*" (Lk. 15: 19). I always sin and do not keep myself.

In all Church Sacraments, is your spirit aware of the grace concealed in every Sacrament, and lives this grace?

Symbols:

There are certain phrases in the Holy Bible, if taken literally, the words of the apostle *"the letter kills"* (2 Cor. 3: 6) will apply to them. But in the spirit you can understand their meaning and what they represent.

The Song of Songs, for example, cannot be understood literally but according to spiritual symbolism

It is the same with many words included in the Holy Bible, such as the words; sword, fire, leaven ... etc. which we mentioned in our articles on "Holy Bible Terminology"

The words of God are spirit and life (Jn. 6: 63)

Thus you understand them with your spirit and turn them into life.

CHAPTER X

THE WILL

THE WILL
How is it strengthened and how weakened?

One often wants to behave well but is not able, or is aware that something is wrong and wishes to avoid it but is not able. The will is weak!

An example of this is the person who is dominated by a certain bad habit which he cannot get rid of. He knows that smoking (for example) is bad for his health, wastes his money, weakens his will and its smell remains in his mouth and teeth. However, he cannot stop smoking. He wants, but is not able as St. Paul put it as if on the mouth of such a person who does what he wants not:

"For what I will to do, that I do not practice; but what I hate, that I do ... But now, it is no longer I who do it, but sin that dwells in me. For I know that in me (that is, in my flesh) nothing good dwells; for to will is present with me, but how to perform what is good I do not find. For the good that I will to do, I do not do; but the evil I will not to do, that I practice. Now if I do what I will not to do, it is no longer I who do it, but sin that dwells in me ... O wretched man that I am! Who will deliver me from this body of death!" (Rom. 7: 15-24).

It is the case of one who is unable to resist sin or to do good. His will is weak in both cases.

Causes for weakness of will:

Here, we shall search for the causes of weakness of the will and how can we strengthen such weakness.

No doubt tendency to good is the origin in man who is created in God's image after His likeness (Gen. 1: 26, 27). Tendency to evil is something exotic which causes we should know.

A person is able -especially with the New Testament grace- to walk in the Lord's way. What then forces him into the way of sin? What weakens his will before sin?

If we consult history, we shall find that our mother Eve, when created by God, had no sin within her. She sinned when she desired to be like God as the devil tempted her (Gen. 3: 5). That lust weakened her will and she could not resist the temptation of the forbidden tree, but rather she "*saw that the tree was good for food, it was pleasant to the eyes, and a tree desirable to make one wise, she took of its fruit and ate*" (Gen. 3: 6).

1. The first thing, then, that makes the will weak is the lust:

Any lust weakens the will, whatever that lust might be; whether lust of the body, lust of money and property, lust of positions and greatness or lust of revenge. The more the lust grows, the harder it presses on the will until the will fails completely, then the words of the apostle are realized, "*the evil I will not to do, that I practice*".

Hence, among the means of strengthening the will, is treatment of one's lusts and removal thereof from the heart.

2. The will is weakened and lust gets more hold when one keeps near to the subject of sin or the causes of sin:

One of the fathers said; when you are far from the subject of sin, you might be fought only from within. But when you are near, you will be fought from two sides; internally & externally and both try to make you fall because you will get weak facing them both.

Therefore, a wise person should keep away from stumbling blocks and from the subject and causes of sin as that his will might not weaken when faced by sin temptations.

Keeping away from the subject of sin includes keeping away from bad company causing you troubles and bringing sinful thoughts into your mind and heart that they press on you and weaken your will. That is why it is written, *"Evil company corrupts good habits"* (1 Cor. 15: 33). Of this evil company the psalmist warns us, *"Blessed is the man who walks not in the counsel of the ungodly, nor stands in the path of sinners, nor sits in the seat of the scornful"* (Ps. 1: 1).

3. The will is more weakened by remaining a long time in the environment of sin:

Haste is important; whether it is haste in forsaking sin, because haste will make your will stronger, or make you hasten in doing good, it makes your will positively stronger.

So, when you are fought by sin and you resist it immediately, not keeping its thoughts within you, your will gets stronger and more able to dismiss that sin.

But if you leave sin grow in your heart, crushing your senses, playing with your emotions, tempting you and convincing your mind, it will by time prevail on you and you will not be able to resist it. Even if you overcome, this will be with great effort and with the interference of grace to save you.

There is a great difference between pulling out sin while still a herb in ground and trying to pull it out after its roots had extended in soil and its stem had risen high in air with branches here and there. It is well said, thus, in the psalm speaking on sin, *"Happy shall he be who takes and dashes your little ones against the rock"* (Ps. 137: 9), and *"That rock was Christ"* (1 Cor. 10: 4).

Whenever a sinful thought occurs to you and you dismiss it quickly, your will get more strength.

But if you open the doors of your mind to it, linger in dismissing it and argue with it letting it remain in your mind for some time, you will have your will weakened before it. You will submit to it, or even if you want to dismiss it afterwards, this will be with great difficulty, and it will easily return to you seeing your lenience with it.!

Making haste in dismissing sin or in performing the commandment is a matter necessary for strengthening the will.

When sin pressed on Joseph the righteous, he fled quickly even though his robe was torn. Had he waited for some time and lingered in flying, who knows what would have happened to him!!

When Lot lingered in going out of the land of Sodom, the two angels urged him to hurry, saying, *"Escape for your life! Do not look behind you nor stay anywhere in the plain. Escape to the mountains, lest you be destroyed"* (Gen. 19: 16, 17).

Long time, remaining in the environment of sin, and hesitation, all this weakens the will. But a person with a strong will hastens in doing good without delay.

Such a person does not wait lest the devil tempts him to rethink over the matter and his mind changes! The devil, to prevent a person from doing good, does not say to him do not do that, but says: wait, think it over, let us discuss for few minutes and I will give you a good counsel! In this way you are lost. Lingering too much in doing good opens the door to the adversary to fight, and how easy it is that your will weakens.

Take for example the lost son.

When he became aware of his bad condition and he thought of repenting, he said, *"I will arise and go to my father, and will say to him: Father, I have sinned against heaven and before you, and I am no longer worthy to be called your son. Make me like one of your hired servants"*, *"And he arose and came to his father"* (Lk. 15: 18-20). Who knows? If he had lingered, what would have happened to his will?

Abraham the patriarch, when God command him to offer his son as a burnt offering, what did he do?

Abraham did not linger at all but *"rose early in the morning"* and took with him his son Isaac, the wood and the knife (Gen. 22: 3). And with will and power he began to carry out the order without any delay. Perhaps, if he waited or changed his mind, there would be wars fighting him! Or even if his will did not weaken, the will of Sarah, Isaac's mother, would weaken. Many hardships would have surrounded him to weaken his will.

When grace moves your will towards good, do not think or discuss the matter, but do it lest the devil takes the opportunity of your hesitation and takes part with you in thinking, thus your will weakens.

Then, the good will you had will faint and might even vanish. Doing good without hesitating shows will power and leads to strengthening of will.

Here are some examples: Suppose you are listening to a sermon or reading a spiritual book or listening to an advice from your father confessor, and it occured to you to reconcile someone you are quarreling with, do not wait, arise immediately and go to reconcile with him. If you wait, your intention might change and you might think it over; why should I go to reconcile with him, why not wait till he comes to me? I accept the principle of reconciliation, but if I go to him, he might think me weak or admitting my fault. So, to keep my dignity, I shall wait till someone mediates between us. This is better. Here the will got weak with regard to taking the initiative and it might end without reconciliation because you lost your will power due to hesitation and discussing!

* When paying the tithes, for example, you might have the will power to pay in the beginning. When you receive your salary, pay the tithes directly, the same as you pay your house rental, or keep the tithes in a special box and call it the Lord's box until you hand over to those who have the right to.

  But if you postpone, you will open a door for wars which might weaken your will regarding paying the tithes. You will find yourself rethinking and discussing the matter with yourself examining your financial needs that month. You might say 'there is a good reason for adjourning paying the tithes. We can pay them afterwards even in monthly instalments, or wait till we receive the yearly increment after some months'. In this way your will is weakened and you do not pay.

* The same happens in the case of resisting sin. When Cain envied his brother Abel and thought of killing him, God warned him, *"sin lies at the door. And its desire is for you, but you should rule over it"* (Gen. 4: 7). The words *"you should rule over it"* means that his will at that time was able to resist that sin, but when he was slow in dismissing it out of his mind and heart, it took hold of him and prevailed on his will, thus leading him to kill his brother.

  Be aware that your sensitive systems are easily affected; whether your mind, your senses, your heart or your emotions. Do not let all these exposed to spiritual wars for a long time or your will gets weak!

4. The will is also weakened when one involves gradually in the atmosphere of sin.

Quick descending can be observed, but gradual and slow descending may not be observed. Perhaps you are not aware that when you travel from Wadi El Natroun -where the monasteries exist- to Cairo or to Alexandria towards the salty lake, you are descending scores of meters on your way.

Likewise, in spiritual life, you might descend gradually from fervor to lukewarmness to coldness, then you fall as your will breaks down while you do not observe how it did weaken gradually!

Be on your guard then, if you reject certain sins automatically and immediately, know then that your will is still powerful.

On the other hand, if you do reject sins immediately but after some thinking or hesitation, know then that your former power has gone and your will is getting weaker.

And if you negotiate with the sinful thought for a while then wake to yourself refusing to continue, know that your will has begun to weaken but did not continue. You have not perfected the fall!

Still if you fell and could not rise or do not want to, know that your will has broken down and has become disabled and need strong quick treatment.

Sin may not fight you directly and boldly so that your will might not reject it. It rather deceives your will gradually.

Sin may even go step by step that you might not be aware of it, and in all this it weakens your will when you accept such a gradual movement until you fall in the pit. The first step that leads you to sin might even not be a sin in itself, but just a deceitful concealed step which gradually deceives your will and when you accept it you lose your first awe. The will power will then get weak till it submits.

What weakens our will, therefore, is that we are not firm or decisive with regard to the first step.

Because of negligence and slackening the will loses its power and takes a weak position, whereas in fighting sin, your will needs take a firm stand to reject it from the very beginning. Negligence, slackening and slowness lead to weakness of will.

Samson the Valiant by graduation and long time weakened before Delilah's pressing. Samson did not reject that persistence in the beginning, and by time his will broke down, he disclosed his secret and his fall was great (Jud. 16).

How can the will be strengthened?

It can be strengthened by various means, among which are the following:

1. Means of grace:

The means of grace strengthens the relationship with God and keeps our thoughts with Him. Thus the will gets strong and dare not submit to sin.

Therefore, if you want to strengthen your will keep always to the means of grace. So long as you always contemplate on the Holy Bible, on prayer, on psalms and hourly prayers, on spiritual songs, praise hymns and meetings, on confessing and partaking of the Holy Communion, you will find yourself encompassed with God's love. Your strong will shall not weaken before sin, for you will have immunity against it.

But if you keep away from spiritual means, you will become spiritually weak, your tendency to good will be less, and your will becomes more responsive to sin. The devil will take the opportunity and attack while your will has no spiritual weapon that strengthens it being away from the inner voice that calls it to God.

Someone might say: I keep to all the spiritual means, I pray and fast, but my will weakens before sin. How can it be?

I say to such a person: You might be practising the means of grace but not in a spiritual way. You read the Holy Bible merely as a duty without any contemplation on it. You pray as a routine without understanding. You go to church meetings as a habit but without getting benefit!! If you practise the means of grace in a spiritual way, certainly this will make your will powerful.

In the scale of life we have two pans; that of God and that of the world.

Sometimes we put much in the pan of the world, so it becomes heavier in weight whereas God's pan remains empty, so it gets lighter. Thus, if you find the world's pan getting heavier, put whatever you can of the means of grace in God's pan till it prevails and in this way your will is strengthened in doing good. You are not standing still, but like the clock's pendulum moving to the right and to the left. The more you force yourself towards God, the more your will becomes more powerful.

Keep yourself always within a spiritual environment that strengthens your will, and keep away from any offending environment that weakens the will.

I will give an example how a person living in a spiritual environment has strong will and how his will weakens when he moves into a bad environment;

St. Peter the apostle: when he was in the spiritual company of the Lord Christ and the apostles, his will was so strong that he said to the Lord, *"Though all become deserters because of You, I will never desert You ... Even though I must die with You, I will not deny You"* (Mt. 26: 33, 35) (Lk. 22: 33). This Peter himself, while in the high priest's courtyard, denied the Lord, cursed and swore he did not know the Man (Mt. 26: 73). His will had weakened or rather collapsed in such an anti Christ atmosphere!!

Another example is the righteous Lot:

When he was in the company of our saintly father Abraham, beside the alter, his will was strong. But when he went to Sodom he lost the two spiritual means -i.e. Abraham and the altar- his will weakened as well as the will of his wife and two daughters. It was said about him that he was overcome by the conduct of the bad people, *"for that righteous man ... tormented his righteous soul ... by seeing and hearing their lawless deeds"* (2 Pet.2: 7, 8).

So important are the spiritual means for strengthening of the will:

The Holy Bible says about the righteous person that he is *"like a tree planted by the rivers of water"* (Ps. 1: 3) i.e. a tree always connected with springs of spiritual nutrition, thus it is fruitful, *"That brings its fruit in its season"* (Ps. 1: 3) Imagine for instance someone whose heart is attached to prayer and spiritual contemplations on the Holy Bible; when such a person is attacked by a bad thought, is it possible that his will weakens before such a thought? Or rather it will be immune against it with the spiritual contemplations!

Let your heart and mind be attached to God so that your will might become strong; for if your mind is distracted away from the means of grace on worldly matters, your will shall certainly weaken.

See what is the environment surrounding you? Does it support your will towards good or weakens it? Do the amusement and recreation means around your strengthen your will and support your resistance of sin, or the opposite? Do the friends and acquaintances with whom you spend your time encourage you to be attached to God and assist you to strengthen your will spiritually, or not?

2. Forcing oneself is also among the means that strengthen the will:

Do you always pamper yourself and give it whatever it desires, as Solomon did, saying, *"Whatever my eyes desired I did not keep from them"* (Eccl. 2: 10)? If so, your will certainly will weaken because it cannot find what controls it. It will lose control over its desire, and you lose control over your will. So, force yourself to do good and to be attached to God. So long as you force yourself firmly into the spiritual way, you will certainly have your will strengthened.

Perhaps you would ask: If I force myself, shall I be in a spiritual status?

Is forced prayer -for instance- a spiritual prayer? I tell you that the love of God which leads you to force yourself is itself a spiritual state.

Forcing oneself is also the first step leading in the end to a spiritual life that has no forcing in it. You might force yourself to do spiritual reading, then you will find pleasure in that and you will continue unforcibly but rather with satisfaction and eagerness. The same can be said about prayer and all spiritual exercises.

Forcing oneself, then, is just the start point but it does not continue like that.

When a small child is sent for the first time to school, he refuses and cries because he will leave his mother's and father's arms, he will miss the love of his relatives and leave the familiar atmosphere to a strange one. So, he goes to school forcibly, but after a while he becomes pleased with the school, with all games and amusement therein and with the new friends and the lessons. So, he longs to be there and press on his mother to dress him to go quickly to the school.

Force yourself to do good, then this will lead you to love good unforcibly and automatically.

Force yourself to forsake sin and your will shall be strengthened and you will reject sin unforecibly afterward.

Force yourself to repent, for this is the spiritual way which St. Paul the apostle advised us to follow when he reprimanded the Hebrews, saying,

"You have not yet resisted to bloodshed, striving against sin" (Heb.12: 4).

The words *"to bloodshed"* mean that you force yourself to resist sin even if this would lead you to be martyred. This means that you should firmly reject whatever temptations sin might offer you and not submit to every thought or desire but to control yourself so that you will might get stronger.

This is like a person who is on a diet. He cannot eat whatever he desires or take much of a certain food he likes. When he thinks of eating a sort of food prohibited by the physician, even a little amount, he refuses firmly and says to himself: the little will lead to the plenty, and this sort will lead to another and to a third. It is better to be firm.

Self-control then leads to strengthening of the will, and when the will is strengthened more self control is attained.

Forced self-control will make the devil get weary of you, seeing you are not easy, and will awe you. And the more you force yourself, God's grace will support and help you because by this you prove that you love God and struggle to walk in His way. God will also respond to your struggling and let His Holy Spirit work within you. Through forcing yourself and through such struggling, you will be aided by the prayers of the saints who cry to God on your behalf that God may help you and not forsake you.

So be obstinate with yourself. But some may ask:
Is obstinacy a sin or a virtue?

If one is obstinate when longing to sin, this obstinacy will be considered a virtue. But if one is obstinate, holding to a sinful thought or behavior, then this obstinacy will be out of pride and insistance on the wrong and thus will be considered double sin.

3. Scrupulousness is also among the means strengthening the will:

It means that your conscience is always awake, never sleeps, not even for a moment. However, in some cases, though the conscience might be awake, the will is weak regarding doing good, or longs to sin and it silences the conscience. It is true that the conscience guides to good works, but it does not force one to do.

4. God's fear and God's love do also strengthen the will:

Through God's fear the will gets strong in keeping away from sin, and through God's love the will gets strong in doing good and righteousness. How is that?

A person who fears God dares not disobey Him. And his fear of doing evil, of God's punishment and of God whom he does not see, all this will strengthen his will to refrain from sinning. Whenever sin is presented to him, he will say, *"How then can I do this great wickedness, and sin against God"* (Gen. 39: 9).

Likewise, a person who loves God, his heart will be inflamed by this love and consequently his will for doing good and for rejecting sin which is not then in conformity with his new nature in the life of holiness.

5. For the will to be strengthened, there should be values which one holds and becomes committed to:

There should be certain values to which a person holds and never forsake under any circumstances. A person may put before him certain values, for example that he never becomes a coward or a betrayer. His will should be strong and hard as steel. Whatever outer pressures might be there, he remains courageous, and never betrays his country, his church, or someone who entrusted him with a secret or a deposit.

The martyrs had such strong will: Faith was among the values they were keen to hold to. Their will never weakened under the tortures they faced.

Someone else holds -for example- to a value: that he steals not. If he steels he despises himself, returns what he stole and never keeps anything not his own. If such a person takes a bus and the fare is not collected from him, he asks for paying it, unlike another person who has no values and in such a case he rejoices for not paying the fare and considers himself lucky for being a friend to the ticket collector. He might be so, but that collector is not the owner of the bus and has no right to exempt anyone from the fare!

Our will might sometimes get weak because some values in our lives have weakened.

On the other hand, if values are strong in our lives and we are strongly committed to them, our will shall be very strong.

There are social as well as religious values, such as; respecting and honoring the elders and teachers. No one dares insult his father or teacher, argues with him, sits while he is standing or hurts his feelings with any word or act. A strong will holds firmly to such values.

There are also different values such as obeying the laws, the public order and respecting the principals. Wherever these values do exist, the will is strongly committed to them. And whenever any of such values weakens, the will is aroused to revolt, protest and disobey.

Religion offers us certain values which strengthen the will to fulfill them.

In fasting -for instance- the will is strong in refraining from eating. So fasting is a means for strengthening the will, and the strong will is a means for practising it.

Among the values also is putting off the shoes before going into the sanctuary. Here the will cannot be so weak as to break this rule, it is firmly committed to it. Some countries who do not have this rule are not worried when not following it.

Thus, one's will is subject to many things which determine its strength or weakness.

One's will is subject to domination of lust and desire, of values and committment thereto, and of self control or liberty. The will is controlled by keeping away from or obeying the commandments and practising the means of grace. It is controlled by the conscience whether awake or sleeping, and by the type of thoughts dominating over the mind. The will is also subject to the extent of one's holding to faith, to one's attachment to God, and to one's obedience to commandments.

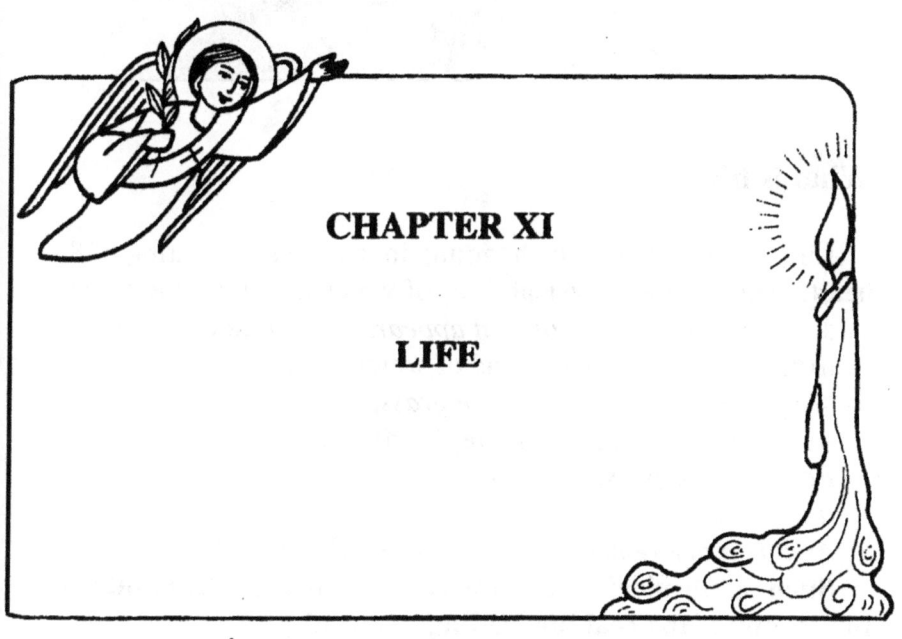

CHAPTER XI

LIFE

WHAT IS LIFE?
And What Is The Kind Of Life We Should Lead?

What is life:

Life is not mere breath going in and out or beating of the heart! This is the physical life of which St. James the apostle said, *"It is even a vapor that appears for a little time and then vanishes away"* (Jas. 4:14), and of which the psalmist said,
"As for man, his days are like grass;
As a flower of the field, so he flourishes.
For the wind passes over it, and
it is gone,
And its place remembers it no more." (Ps. 103: 15, 16)
Such a physical life is a period of estrangement and test, but its aim is the real life leading to eternity.

What is the real life then? And how can we attain it?

At the concluding chapters of the gospel, St. John the beloved alone, after recording the miracles of the Lord Christ, tells us about it. He says, *"But these are written that you may believe that Jesus is the Christ, the Son of God, and that believing you may have life in His name"* (Jn. 20: 31).

What does it mean *"you may have life"*?

The same phrase was said by the Lord Christ Himself before that, when He said, *"I have come that they may have life"* (Jn. 10: 10). Those of whom the Lord was speaking had lives according to the flesh, but the Lord did not mean that. He meant another kind of life which His apostle John also meant. What then is the kind of that life?

It is evident that not every living person is considered alive. See what the Lord said to the angel of the Church in Sardis, *"You have a name that you are alive, but you are dead"* (Rev. 3: 1).

A sinner is a dead person even though he is alive.

This is what the father said about the lost son who repented and came back, *"for this my son was dead and is alive again"* (Lk. 15: 24) He meant that his son was dead while in sin, and he became alive when he repented. In the same meaning, St. Paul the apostle says *"And you ... were dead in trespasses and sins"* (Eph. 2: 1) and also, *"even when we were dead in trespasses, made us alive together with Christ"* (Eph. 2: 5)

We have obtained life by the salvation presented us by the Lord Christ.

It is the eternal life of which the Lord said, *"that whoever believes in Him should not perish but have eternal life"* But what is the real life which we should attain here on the earth? St. Paul the apostle says in this regard,
"For to me, to live is Christ" (Phil. 1: 21).

Indeed, Christ is the Life. Did he not say to Martha the sister of Lazarus, *"I am the resurrection and the life"* (Jn. 11: 25), and say to His disciples, *"I am the way, the truth, and the life"* (Jn. 14: 6). In the gospel written by St. John the Lord Christ was described as *"In Him was life"* (Jn. 1: 4).

Since Christ is the Life, whoever abides in Him abides in life and becomes, spiritually speaking, a human being. How deep indeed are the words said by St. Paul the apostle on this point!
"It is no longer I who live, but Christ lives in me" (Gal. 2: 20).

Another meaning of life is the dwelling of the Holy Spirit in us in such a manner that our lives become under the leadership of the Holy Spirit, as it said, *"For as many as are led by the Spirit of God, these are sons of God"* (Rom. 8: 14).

The Lord Christ told about some of the work of the Holy Spirit within us, He said, *"for it is not you who speak, but the Spirit of your Father who speaks in you"* (Mt. 10: 20).

As for the dwelling of the Holy Spirit within us, the apostle said, *"Do you not know that you are the temple of God and that the Spirit of God dwells in you?"* (1 Cor. 3: 16).

Hence, the true real life is the life of the believer who is a temple of God where the Lord Christ lives and the Holy Spirit dwells.

About this relationship of the believer with God, the Lord Christ says, *"If anyone loves Me, ... and My Father will love him and we will come to him and make Our home with him*" (Jn. 14: 23).

It means that the believer becomes a home for the Father and the Son, besides being a temple for the Holy Spirit. He becomes a dwelling place for the Holy Trinity! How deep indeed such a life with God would be!!

If for us life is Christ (Phil. 1: 21), what happens within us and to us?

Since Christ lives in us, therefore whatever we do is done by Christ in us. This conforms with what the apostle said, "*it is no longer I ..., but Christ ...*" Then we cannot sin (1 Jn. 3: 9). We live the real life and afterwards we attain the eternal life where we can eat of the Tree of Life (Rev. 2: 7) and where the Lord gives us the Crown of Life (Rev. 2: 10).

How can we attain such a life?

1. This real life begins with faith on being baptized.

In baptism we die with the Lord Christ to rise with Him also as the apostle says, "*buried with Him in baptism, in which you also were raised with Him ...*" (Col. 2: 12) (Rom. 6: 2-5). In baptism our old man is crucified that the body of sin might be done away with (Rom. 6: 6). And when our old man dies, another new man rises in the likeness of the Lord Christ. The apostle says on this point:

"*For as many of you as were baptized into Christ have put on Christ*" (Gal. 3: 27).

You have put on the righteousness of Christ in that new man who rose with Christ in baptism to walk in the newness of life or in the new life. In baptism also, you have put on the life in Christ. How is that? Since life is getting rid of death, so in your death with Christ in baptism, you get rid of the judgment of death issued against you and you come into life.

2. You attain the real life by repentance also.

On the importance of repentance the Lord said, *"Unless you repent you will all likewise perish"* (Lk. 13: 3, 5). Perdition is the loss of life, therefore it is written in the Acts *"God has also granted to the gentiles repentance to life"* (Acts 11: 18), and *"Repent therefore and be converted that your sins may be blotted out"* (Acts 3: 19).

Since the wages of sin is death (Rom. 6: 23), then repentance is the way to life. In repentance man gets rid of the love of the world, being aware that *"friendship with the world is enmity with God"* (Jas. 4: 4), and that, *"If anyone loves the world, the love of the Father is not in him"* (1 Jn.2: 15). That is why the church has arranged in the readings in every Mass the words of the apostle, *"Do not love the world or the things in the world ... And the world is passing away, and the lust of it"* (1 Jn. 2: 15,17)

3. Hence the real life, from the negative aspect, is forsaking of sin, and from the positive aspect, is walking in the Spirit.

As the apostle said, *"There is therefore now no condemnation to those who are in Christ Jesus who ... walk ... according to the*

Spirit" (Rom. 8: 1), and, *"For to be carnally minded is death, but to be spiritually minded is life and peace"* (Rom. 8: 6). The real life is in the care for the spirit so that we might come to the rule that:

One's body is led by one's spirit, and one's spirit is led by God's Spirit.

This is the true life as the psalmist says;
"Who is the man who desires life,
....
*The eyes of the Lord are on the righteous
And His ears are open to their cry" (Ps. 34: 12-15)*

And the Lord says at the end of the Book of Deuteronomy, *"See, I have set before you today life and good, death and evil ... therefore choose life, that you and your descendants may live; that you may love the Lord your God ... for He is your life ..."* (Deut. 30: 15, 19, 20).

Since God is your life, keeping away from Him is keeping away from life.

4. Partaking of the Holy communion in the Eucharist Sacrament is another means to attain life.

The Lord Christ says, *"I am the bread of life"*, *"I am the bread which came down from heaven ... and the bread that I shall give is My flesh which I shall give for the life of the world"*, *"Most assuredly, I say to you, ... whoever eats My flesh and drinks My blood has eternal life, and I will raise him at the last day."*, *"For My flesh is food indeed, and My blood is drink indeed ... abides in Me and I in him"*, *"he who feeds on Me will live because of Me"*, and, *"He who eats this bread will live forever"* (Jn. 6: 41-58).

Do you take your spiritual nutrition in the Eucharist Sacrament? And do you take it deservedly? Remember the words of the apostle *"whoever eats this bread or drinks this cup of the Lord in an unworthy manner will be guilty of the body and blood of the Lord"*, *"eats and drinks judgment to himself"* (1 Cor. 11: 27, 29).

5. Another means for obtaining life is the spiritual nutrition, especially the word of God.

The Lord said, *"Man shall not live by bread alone, but by every word that proceeds from the mouth of God"* (Mt. 4: 4) (Deut. 8: 3), and also, *"Do not labor for the food which perishes, but for the food which endures to everlasting life"* (Jn. 6: 27).

So, let everyone work in order to obtain the spiritual food which qualifies us for the eternal life, which food the Lord described by the words, *"The words that I speak to you are spirit and they are life"* (Jn. 6: 63). Understand the spirituality of the word and turn it into a life for you.

When some of the disciples left the Lord, He said to the twelve, *"Do you also want to go away?"*. But St. Peter the apostle said to Him, *"Lord, to whom shall we go? You have the words of eternal life."* (Jn. 6: 68). So, be keen, my brother, on holding to the word of life.

Be keen also to practise all the spiritual means which are the source of life. Be keen on contemplation and spiritual reading and meetings and on reading the stories of the saints of which the fathers said they are like water for newly planted seedlings.

As for God's words: meditate in it day and night (Josh. 1: 8) (Ps. 1: 2). *"Shall be in your heart ... teach them diligently to your children ... talk of them when you sit in your house ..."* (Deut. 6: 6, 7)

A fruitful life:

A living person is the one whose life has a message to perform however short his life on earth might be. In this way one's life becomes fruitful and productive.

The life of God's children is not measured by the length but by the depth.

John the Baptist:

He served only for one year, but he was able to prepare the way before the Lord and make His paths straight. Thus he deserved to be the greatest born of women (Mt. 11: 11). He ended his life as a martyr after testifying to the truth, reprimanding king Herod (Mt. 14: 3-12).

Stephen the first deacon:

He was mere deacon, not priest or bishop. He served for a short time, but his life was fruitful. No sooner had the hands been laid on him than *"the word of God spread and the number of the disciples multiplied greatly in Jerusalem"* (Acts 6: 7, 8). The reason of his successful life was his being full of Holy Spirit, wisdom, and faith. (Acts 6: 3, 5). He was martyred and deserved to see the Lord Christ standing at the right hand of God (Acts 7: 55). His face was as the face of an angel (Acts 6: 15).

Now, is your life fruitful? What work have you done for which you deserve a crown?

Some people obtained the crown of celibacy or chastity. Others obtained the crown of struggling or martyrdom, or the crown of monasticism, the crown of priesthood, the crown of righteousness or other crowns.

What is then **your** crown? If you have fruit which is worth *"Hold fast what you have that no one may take your crown"* (Rev. 3: 11), *"else I will come ... and remove your lampstand from its place"* (Rev. 2: 5). Hearken to the words of the Holy Bible, *"every tree which does not bear good fruit is cut down and thrown into the fire"* (Mt. 3: 10).

Let your life be fruitful for the kingdom and for the society you live in. Let it be fruitful in virtue and ministry, and let the fruit be continual.

A continual extended life:

It is like the life of the fathers and saints whose fruit of life and struggle is still alive in the church after their departure from this mortal world, giving benefit to all people, whether those fathers were good examples or heroes of faith.

Among those saints is Athanasius the apostolic

His life did not end with his death, but is still extending along generations through his theological writings in defence of faith against the Arians.

The life of St. John Chrysostom also is extending and works in our generation, as it has done in past generations, through his sermons and deep commentaries of the Holy Bible.

Time is lacking for speaking of the many saints whose fruitful life continued to work for long generations such as that of St. Cyril the great, St. Basil, St. Gregory, and St. Savirus of Antioch.

There are also the great fathers of the desert whose life is still extending in monasticism throughout the whole world like St. Anthony the great, St. Bachum who laid down the laws of monasticism, and St. Paul the first anchorite. Have their lives ended by their death? Certainly not.

The same may be said about the saints of repentance.

Those left us a live example of return to God through true repentance which continued to grow till it turned into a deep life of holiness. Among those are St. Moses the black, St. Augustine, St. Mary the Coptic and many others.

Other saints have extended lives through the intercession and help they offer us.

An example of those are St. Virgin Mary, St. George and others, who -after their departure- are still entrusted by God to do some helping services for the people still alive on the earth. Have the lives of those ended by their departure form this mortal world? Or still continuing in our generations and in future ones?

It is just a simple idea about the real life which was fruitful on the earth and extended after the departure to the other world. It is an example for all of us.

Table of Contents

	Page
Introduction	5
Chapter 1: Man Is Soul, Body & Spirit	9
Chapter 2: Man's Capabilities & Instincts	29
Chapter 3: How Is Man's Life Managed?	53
Chapter 4: The Mind	65
Chapter 5: The Conscience	85
Chapter 6: The Body	101
Chapter 7: The Heart	113
Chapter 8: Thoughts	139
Chapter 9: The Human Spirit	163
Chapter 10: The Will	191
Chapter 11: Life	211

www.ingramcontent.com/pod-product-compliance
Lightning Source LLC
Chambersburg PA
CBHW061430040426
42450CB00007B/978